Man
by Nature

The Hidden Programming
Controlling Human Behavior

Adam Leonard

Egress Publishing
Sarasota, FL

Egress Publishing

Copyright © 2006, 2008, 2009 by Adam Leonard
All rights reserved. Published by Egress Publishing
Previously published by:
Peppertree Press under ISBN: 978-1-934246-07-8
TRIAD Publishing Group under ISBN: 978-0-9796994-8-1

ISBN 13: 978-0-6152802-5-7
ISBN 10: 0-6152802-5-0
Printed in the U.S.A.
Printed March 2009

To Shirley belovéd,
my Muse, my Wife, my Love, my Life

Table of Contents

Introduction:
This (Epochal) Moment in Time

"When we remember we are all mad, the mysteries disappear and life stands explained." – Mark Twain

Why can't we all just live in peace?

Because it's not our nature; because we're not programmed that way.

Evidence has been mounting steadily that human behavior is extensively programmed and that our chronic human ills stem from this programming. We're now approaching a turning point in human history, the point at which Mankind finally acquires sufficient understanding of its own nature to begin diminishing its self-destructive behavior. This book is a step toward that understanding: it is a serious effort to convince you that despite the illusion of being consciously in control of your behavior, much of that behavior stems from unconscious "programming," and the illusion that you are consciously in control is *itself* part of the programming.

Before dismissing this as the mad mutterings of a demented soul, consider this reality: the entire history of Man is a history of war and strife; we build up only to tear down, and cry, "Peace, peace!" only to wage war. If Man were rational, this would be unfathomable. Why would we rationally choose to kill one another, and live in fear of being killed, rather than rationally choosing to live in peace and harmony? It's only when we allow the possibility that Man is irrational, that we are driven to war in some unconscious way, that our behavior – perversely – begins to make sense.

Not only our history, but classic literature and drama also instruct us that Man is flawed: Homer and Virgil, Dante and Shakespeare, Arthur Miller and Chaim Potak, all have chronicled Man's persistent – and consistent – irrationalities. From Achilles to Macbeth to Willy Loman, flawed heroes are shown succumbing to passions they're unaware of, and irrationally destroying themselves and the things they love most. Only if we allow the possibility that Man is not rational, does this begin to make sense.

It has long been taught that we are doomed to repeat past tragedies if we don't remember history. The emerging reality is more severe: even if we remember history we are *still* doomed to repeat it unless we become cognizant of the underlying factors in our nature that provoke our behavior. And to date, little is known about our nature. All we have are unproved theories and a greater lust for fighting over them than for finding the truth.

If you think otherwise, if you're impressed with the vast libraries on philosophy, sociology, psychology, and psychiatry, try this: Take all that is known about Man's nature and show how it can be used to resolve even one of Man's recurring problems. Can it prevent wars? Can it cure hatreds in the Middle East? The Balkans? Africa? Can it resolve racial strife? Can it end inner-city gang wars? Can it eliminate drug addiction or alcoholism? Can it pacify soccer fans or Little League parents? Can it end marital strife, make peace between you and your family, you and yourself?

If it can ... why hasn't it?

No, the truth is that all our philosophies, all our efforts to end wars, all our struggles to understand and improve ourselves, all have failed because they have been based on the assumption that we are *rational* ... that, unless insane, the things we do are things we consciously decide to do.

That assumption, always false, is no longer defensible. The evidence against "rational Man" has become too great to ignore. Over the preceding century various pieces of the puzzle have dropped into place, and now the ongoing studies in neuroscience on how the brain functions have provided sufficient critically needed pieces for the hidden truth to become discernible: We are *programmed* to behave the way we do; we are *programmed* to be consciously unaware of our programming; we will *continue* behaving the way we do, even unto destruction, until the reality of our hidden programming becomes acknowledged, accepted, and acted upon.

This, then, is an introductory text to our hidden programming ... to *your* programming and mine. If you have the fortitude and tenacity to read this through, it will explain to you much about yourself because it will explain much about the human race, or as Samuel L. Clemens (a.k.a. Mark Twain) put it, "the *Damned* Human Race." That unparalleled American author – who penned such memorable lines as "Man is the only animal that blushes, or needs to," and "They too are members of the Human Race; I can speak worse of no man" – observed Man's behavior and marveled at it. He lamented it, lampooned it, and attempted heroically to change it. He began in humor and ended, necessarily, in diatribe, for only diatribe has the remotest chance of altering human beliefs or behavior.

His pessimism was justified, for our internal resistance to examining our beliefs has proven to be the most powerful force within us, stronger even than our urges to live and procreate. Thus we willingly die – and kill – for our beliefs, and no persons on Earth are more despised – or doomed – than the apostates, heretics, and prophets who question established beliefs.

Thus, the biggest obstacle to improving the human race can easily be identified: it is *You and I, and our existing beliefs.* We come equipped with a certitude that we and our groups – national, political, religious, philosophical, whatever – are not part of the problem, but that all competing groups are, and if they would only cooperate with *Us*, peace would reign. That, as you will see, is the way we're wired to feel and believe; we can't help it. The question becomes, then, are we prepared to give up our beloved beliefs and treasured tenets if the unfolding reality of human nature reveals them to be unwise? Are we able and willing to set aside the clichés, dogmas, and mindsets that bind us to our various groups, and make an honest effort to reexamine the nature of Man?

Unfortunately, the evidence indicates that honesty is not Man's strong suit. Diogenes has met both you and me ... and is still searching. When Shakespeare's Mercutio cried, "A plague on both your houses!" he might better have lamented, "A plague on *all* our houses!" Whether we consider ourselves liberals or conservatives, intellectuals or workers, religious or scientific, members of minorities or not, we all have much to answer for. The self-satisfying conviction that we and those with whom we agree are the solution rather than part of the problem wilts rapidly in the sunlight of honest examination. If we truly want to be part of the solution to the human dilemma, we must allow the accruing knowledge of our hidden programming to accomplish what Sam Clemens' bitter tears could not, a painful and humbling reexamination of our favored philosophies and "sacred beliefs."

Our philosophies and beliefs, you see, are *hypotheses*. They are *theories* of what our human nature may be, and of what human behavior is consequently required to fulfill our human needs and desires. The entrenched warfare between competing groups, particularly our "liberals" and "conservatives," on how best to meet human needs is a direct result of the underlying disagreement on what our human nature really *is*, and consequently what our human needs really *are*. Thus it is easy for various groups – each trying to improve human existence based on their own conception of human needs – to become convinced that the other, disagreeing groups have no concern for the common weal but are pursuing selfish goals. Only the ultimate revealing of our "true" nature and the hidden programming that drives it will resolve the conflicts.

The ultimate revealing of our true nature will be a long time coming – beyond our lifetimes – and each facet will be long and viciously fought over by many groups before being accepted as Truth. Nonetheless, now that the nature of the struggle is being revealed, now that we can no longer pretend it is a battle between our (*true*) philosophy and their (*false*) philosophy rather than a battle between *all* our philosophies and the truth about our nature, the question still remains: Are you able and willing to set aside the clichés, dogmas, and mindsets that bind you to your various groups, and make an honest effort to reexamine the nature of Man? ... How you respond to the material in this book will be your answer.

Some words about this book itself are in order: On what science is the "hidden programming" hypothesis based? What are my qualifications to present such a hypothesis? Why have I chosen to write in a nonacademic style? Where do I imagine this treatise to be in the grand scheme of things?

This book – and any other treatise seriously considering human nature – is and must be based on a distillation of the most recent, generally accepted findings in the life sciences. Since humans, *Homo sapiens*, have ascended through many evolutionarily lower life forms, all of the life sciences provide useful input toward understanding human biological underpinnings. Those disciplines studying the brains and behavior of higher animals, of course, provide the most direct and compelling information.

Because these disparate scientific fields employ highly specialized procedures, technologies, and terminologies, it's not possible to be completely knowledgeable and conversant in many fields at once; even most *scientists* are knowledgeable and conversant in only their own. Fortunately, since all the disciplines regularly produce a few scientists who are not only competent in their fields but gifted with the ability to write popular summaries of their work, it *is* possible to keep abreast of the salient findings in a variety of disciplines. Reading these published scientists' works in books and science magazines allows even nonscientists to acquire a reasonable overview of where Science is and where it's heading. Having a natural interest in the life sciences, I have for decades gleaned published works for the latest findings in, among others: anthropology, ethnology, evolutionary biology, molecular biology, neuroscience, psychiatry, psychobiology, psychology, and zoology. This book is based almost entirely upon a piecing together of that gleaned knowledge.

Concerning my qualifications to propose a "hidden programming" hypothesis: I was a software engineer (a.k.a. computer programmer) for most of my working life and can convincingly claim to be familiar with programming at all its levels. This familiarity made it inevitable, as I followed neuroscience's discoveries involving human behavior and the brain, that I should entertain the idea that nearly *all* human behavior – especially the irrational – was traceable to "programming" in the brain. That idea, which eventually grew to become this book, is original only in its scope. Many people have portrayed various brain functions and specific behaviors as "programmed," and the quest in both science and science fiction to achieve "artificial intelligence" through programming legitimizes the possibility that if programming might emulate us, then we ourselves might be programmed. To the best of my knowledge, however, no one has hypothesized and detailed a sweeping overview of the programming that controls *all* human behavior. This book does exactly that, and I contend that once this programming has been described to you, you will begin to observe it everywhere, further validating its aptness.

As you read this book, it will become obvious that I have chosen to write in a nonacademic style. Although claiming to be advancing a hypothesis based on scientific findings, I provide none of the footnotes and few of the references expected in scientific and academic papers. This is deliberate and necessary for four very good reasons:

First, examining human nature requires distilling information from so many fields that documenting it all would result in so lengthy and boring a treatise no one would read it ... particularly since most of the disciplines have differing schools within them, and attempting to give fair representation to all sides would *really* make it long and boring!

Second, academia itself has so many superstitions and artificial barriers within and between disciplines that it's unwise to adopt their ways when addressing human nature. As an example, those in disciplines dealing with animal behavior are straitjacketed with an acute fear of anthropomorphism. Anyone remotely suggesting a "human-like" quality in the behavior of a lesser animal is subject to such ridicule that his best bet is to seek another line of work. It simply isn't admissible that as Man ascended the evolutionary path, he may well have retained many of the "lower-animal" mechanisms and layered his new abilities atop them, and that consequently it's quite *likely* some "human-like" behavior will be observed in lower animals because it's really "lower-animal" behavior retained in us. Alas, the sad truth is that many in the "scientific" disciplines have wandered into reverse superstition ... believing with insufficient evidence that things not explainable by current theories are not "unknown," but are patently "false" and should be rejected with as much fanfare as possible. Apostates and heretics are no more appreciated in Science than in Religion. You'd almost think they were run by the same species.

Third, there is a gulf, or at least a moat, between scientific disciplines. If you're a scientist or social scientist, publishing a paper extrapolating insights from your own field into anybody else's is a sure ticket to professional censure and public derision. Sorry, but a carpenter's card doesn't allow you to do electrical work, and the order of business is to dismantle you first and ... well, actually that's the *only* order of business. Hence, only fools and un-anointed philosophers attempt to draw together threads from different disciplines and weave speculative essays on the nature of Man.

Finally, the most compelling reason to abandon all pretense of an academic approach is that it's ineffective. As you will see in the following chapters, we simply don't respond to mere facts. Like the mule in the fable of the mule and the two-by-four, it's first necessary to get our attention. There is good reason to suspect that our behavior-controlling programs (whatever and wherever they may be) can't be modified by mere exposure to new information unless there's an accompanying jolt of emotional content, the more traumatic the better. If this suspicion is true, I could present to you all the facts in the world and you might even agree with most of them, but you wouldn't alter any but your most superficial behavior until and unless you experienced them viscerally. Hence, Samuel L. Clemens resorted to diatribe, and I on occasion resort to slightly more inflammatory language than is approved by academia.

Where do I see this treatise in the grand scheme of things? A mere beginning, hardly the whole truth. While I'm certain the "hidden programming" hypothesis has merit as a useful next step in understanding and predicting human behavior, it necessarily is incomplete pending further advances in knowledge, and some of the current assertions undoubtedly will prove to be wrong. Nonetheless, it should provide a needed impetus toward overcoming the self-destructive myths and impulses that have held Mankind in thrall ... forever.

• • •

In the material to follow, the first three chapters provide necessary background information. Chapter 1, *Programmed Man*, demonstrates that programming analogous to that in electronic computers exists within us, and that the analogy is useful in describing human behavior; Chapter 2, *Deluded Man*, presents the neuroscientific evidence supporting the claim that our programming creates the illusion we're in conscious control of our behavior when we are not; and Chapter 3, *Biased Man*, provides additional neuroscientific evidence demonstrating how our programming constantly, unconsciously, and severely biases our thinking.

Chapter 4, *Tribal Man*, is the central and pivotal chapter of this book. It describes the overarching "tribal template" that causes all humans, everywhere, to form tribes and subtribes and to contend with one another. After reading it you'll never again have to ask, "Why can't we all just live in peace?" ... You will know.

Chapters 5 through 12 describe other interesting facets of our programmed behavior that operate within the tribal template to make us the peculiar creatures we are.

And finally, Chapter 13, *Evolving Man*, considers the odds of Man ever evolving sufficiently to overcome his self-destructive programming ... and what steps might be necessary to achieve this miracle.

Chapter 1
Programmed Man:
The Three Levels of Human
Programming

"It is not worthwhile to try to keep history from repeating itself, for man's character will always make the preventing of the repetitions impossible." – Mark Twain

Once you realize Man is not rational, things begin to make sense. Once you realize Man is *programmed* to behave in particular, even peculiar ways, impervious to and in defiance of reason, you can begin to understand his behavior. Until you do, Man's penchant for war and dissension over peace and harmony will remain a mystery to you, and your quixotic efforts to improve the world will only result in a trail of broken windmills.

Make no mistake, we are programmed, as surely and completely as all other living things. Were it possible to place a group of humans "with no history" in isolation anywhere in the world, they would recreate a typical human society as surely as other mammals, birds, fish, and insects recreate theirs.

You may scoff, of course, at such heresy ... at the notion that we, the be-all and end-all of Creation, could be mere machines, endlessly executing a script we didn't write and can edit but sparingly. Scoff while you can; the notion is here to stay, and eventually will be accepted as a fair description of reality.

"Well, just how does this imagined 'programming' work?" you ask. Read on, and I'll show you – first, by describing the levels of programming that exist in computers, and then by identifying analogous levels of programming that exist in ... *You.*

Computers, of course, are "machines": they have physical components that enable them to accept data, perform logical operations upon it, and store or display the results. In the beginning they were mechanical marvels. Later they became behemoths of wires, resisters, capacitors, and vacuum tubes, occasionally spitting fire. Today they're microchips – microscopic circuitry etched into silicon wafers, merely breathing heat. Tomorrow, who knows? Optical, molecular, and biological implementations are already being devised.

Regardless, from the earliest days of electronic computers until this writing, the programming controlling them has been implemented in three ways, forming three levels:

- Hardwired
- Firmwired
- Softwired

The terms, tributes to the days when instructions were actually wired rather than etched or written in memory, are descriptive of the plasticity associated with each method – how hard or easy it is to change the programming once it's written. Hardwired programming can't be changed – it's as permanent as the machine itself; firmwired programming can be changed, but with difficulty – special effort is needed; softwired programming can be changed easily.

These three levels of programming arose naturally as tradeoffs between the flexibility, speed, and cost of the storage mediums involved: Hardwired programming is etched right into a computer's microchip, providing very fast execution speed at a high cost. Firmwired programming is "burned" with special equipment onto high-speed memory chips at a moderate cost; the chips can be rewritten but only by using special equipment and significant time. Softwired programming is written and rewritten quickly and easily onto ordinary, relatively cheap memory chips, but the execution speed is comparatively slow. Consequently, the lowest-level programming that defines the essence of a computer and executes continuously is hardwired; the programming that provides special capabilities (improved performance, additional functionality, handling of specialized devices) is firmwired; and the programs the computer simply "runs" is softwired – written into and executed from ordinary memory.

That succinctly summarizes the whys and wherefores for the three levels of programming typically found in computers. Can anything analogous be seen in Man? The answer is that, yes, Man's discernible programming can readily be grouped into three "levels" based upon the permanency of the programming, how easy or difficult it is to change. The list on the following page provides a sample catalog of our human programming divided into those three levels. Each item will be described in more detail shortly, but first we need to review what is presently known about the "computer" that implements human programming: the brain.

The Three Levels of Human Programming:

Hardwired Human Programming (Unchangeable)
- automatic life-sustaining processes
- species behavior
- scheduled development processes
- instinctive fears
- instinctive behavior manifested as taboos
- Jung's archetypal templates
- gene-based natures, talents, proclivities, susceptibilities, etc.

Firmwired Human Programming (Changeable Only With Effort)
- behavior learned through scheduled development processes
- surviving and coping behavior learned in childhood
- surviving and coping behavior learned with accompanying trauma
- subconscious memory
- beliefs
- addictive behavior
- ingrained habits

Softwired Human Programming (Changeable)
- superficial habits
- knowledge gained through observation and experience
- knowledge gained through being taught
- knowledge deduced or extrapolated from existing knowledge

Interestingly enough, our brains are often described by neuroscientists as being "three brains in one," a concept first proposed in 1952 by Dr. Paul MacLean and later much expanded upon. This "triune brain" description, however, has nothing to do with differing mediums or processing speeds, as in computers, but to their having evolved during three different eons of evolution. Just as an embryo's development reflects its species' anatomical evolution, the triune brain reflects three significant stages of brain evolution: reptilian, early mammalian, and late mammalian, with each stage "layered on top of" and physically enveloping the previous one.

Thus, our "innermost," "oldest" brain controls functions allowing us to exist on the level of lizards; our "middle," "later" brain adds functionality raising mammals above reptiles; and our "outermost," "newest" brain adds functionality raising primates above other mammals. This fifty-year-old generalization is reasonably workable, but in practice requires exceptions and modifications whenever specific functions are examined. Any programmer or engineer will tell you that patching new capabilities onto existing systems is tricky business, and that's true even for Mother Nature. The primitive means of handling the four F's – feeding, fighting, fleeing, and fornicating – couldn't be removed while new functionality was evolving, so the new functionality had to accept its existence and augment rather than remove it. Thus the many contentions between our primitive urges and our more cerebral ones.

It would be nice to be able to claim that our "hardwired," "firmwired," and "softwired" programming mapped directly onto the three major brain divisions, but such is not the case. It's *probably* true that most of our hardwired programming (unconscious, life-sustaining) resides in the "oldest" portion of our brain. It's also *probably* true that most of our softwired programming (conscious, learned) resides in the "newest" portion. But it's probably *not* true that our firmwired programming resides primarily in any one portion. It's more *likely* true that as newer portions of the brain evolved, connections with the older portions enabled augmenting existing functions, and thus many brain functions will be found to be distributed throughout the triune brain, some predominantly in one, some predominantly in another, but others more distributed.

So how is programming implemented in brains – ours and others?

Not in the same way as in computers. The only comparison between the way brains are programmed and the way computers are programmed is that ... well, they're both programmed. Computer designers salivate in envy over the capabilities of the brain. While there are specific kinds of computations that computers can perform faster and better than the human brain, as a general-purpose problem solver the human brain is light-years beyond computers. That's why teams of neuroscientists and computer scientists are working overtime trying to discover and emulate how the brain works its wonders.

We're reluctant to experiment on our own brains, of course, but since Nature is notoriously parsimonious and reuses whatever works, nearly all animal brain circuitry evolved over the millennia is based on the same basic brain cell – the neuron – and the same electrochemical means of interconnection and communication between neurons. Thus, slugs and squid, cats and dogs, mice and monkeys have brain cells similar to Man's, and we can experiment on their brains to learn about brain functions in ways we're reluctant to do on our own.

The basic structure and functioning of brain neurons has become almost common knowledge thanks to widespread interest in understanding drugs and drug addictions. The simplest rendition is: Each neuron cell consists of a central body (soma) having a multitude of branching, hair-like input fibers (dendrites) at one end and a long single output fiber (axon) which branches into a "tree" of output fibers at the other. The dendrites receive input signals from other neurons; the soma "sums" the signals; and if the sum reaches some threshold value, an output signal is sent down the axon tree to trigger outputs to other neurons. The number of inputs and outputs for a given neuron varies widely depending upon its use – anywhere from a few, to hundreds, to thousands.

Within a neuron, signals are transmitted electrically via ion charges, but between neurons, signals are transmitted chemically via "messenger chemicals" (neurotransmitters). Instead of a physical connection between neurons, the tips of the output axons and input dendrites simply "almost touch," and the small gap (synapse) between them is transited by the messenger chemicals. (The well-publicized role some neurotransmitters play in addictions is what has made basic brain cell functioning so widely known.) This two-medium method of transmitting brain signals seems cumbersome at first, but it's actually quite elegant: it provides the brain with a remarkable ability to rewire itself, something that direct physical connections between neurons would not provide.

Reverse engineering our brain to emulate its functioning seemed at first a daunting but doable task: learn how neurons work in small, simple brains and steadily scale up to larger, more complex brains. (The squid, we're told, not only has a lot fewer neurons than humans but ones that are obligingly larger and easier to work with.) It was once expected that neurons would be akin to the simple switches employed in computers, where two inputs are compared to produce a single output, and all inputs and outputs are simply "on" or "off" ... 1's or 0's.

The reality that neurons could have hundreds, even thousands of inputs and outputs radically increased our apprehension of the task, and then it turned out that the electrochemical processing going on at the synapses was manyfold more complex than first thought. For example, there can be synapses not only between axons and dendrites but also between axons and somas, axons and axons, and dendrites and dendrites; chemical messengers can invoke inhibitory (summed negatively) as well as excitatory (summed positively) effects on the receiving entity; different receiving entities can treat signals received from the same neuron differently, sometimes based on the history of what they've received before.

Additionally, it has been found that the "newest" portion of our brain (the neocortex) has six layers (distinguished by the type of neurons predominant in each layer) and that vertical columns of these neurons, crossing all six layers, are tightly interconnected to form microscopic circuits. These "microcircuits" are now viewed as the fundamental processing units in the neocortex. Each microcircuit acts like a "parallel processor" (in computer terminology) that can handle multiple programming tasks simultaneously, so the neocortex acts like a massive array of general-purpose parallel processors, groups of which can be customized for particular functions and – most remarkably – can be rewired on the fly (within limits) to adapt to changing requirements. Adjacent columns in a given area of the neocortex work in parallel – literally as well as functionally – on different aspects of complex tasks.

Clearly, the complexity of the brain is mind boggling, and so is the brain's computational size. Neuroscientists are fond of quoting facts to impress the latter upon us: a cubic *millimeter* of cortex may contain three to four *kilometers* of axons, fifty *thousand* neurons, three hundred *million* interconnections; the entire cortex may contain ten to fifteen *billion* neurons, with sixty *trillion* connections; etc. – I think we get the point. As I said, human computer designers can only salivate with envy. Emulating the brain's methods of programming may prove more than daunting, it may prove impossible. Nonetheless, challenges are what humans like best, and the work is afoot.

● ● ●

Now, having reviewed what is currently known about our brain's basic functioning, let's consider in more detail the three levels of programming it hosts, starting with our hardwired programming.

Hardwired Human Programming (Unchangeable)
• *Automatic Life-Sustaining Processes*

Except for perhaps a few meditation gurus, we exercise no conscious control over our automatic life-sustaining processes – our reflexes, breathing, blood flow, digestion, etc. – nor do we want to. We acknowledge that some internal, subconscious process monitors our vital signs and, when working properly, adjusts and tweaks our body chemistry to achieve optimum performance, very much like the automated control programs monitoring complex industrial operations and power plants. Thus we're almost forced to admit that our automatic life-sustaining processes are programmed. That's good, for it makes us pause a bit before dismissing the notion that we're also programmed in areas we'd like to believe are under our conscious control. ... Or, at least it should.

• *Species Behavior*

As suggested previously, were it possible to place a group of humans "with no history" in isolation anywhere in the world, they would recreate a typical human society as surely as other mammals, birds, fish, and insects recreate theirs. All species are hardwired to behave in their own particular way, and human beings are not exceptions. We copulate, form tribes, and war with one another as naturally – and unconsciously – as any other territorial animal. Microbiologists have demonstrated that about 98 percent of human DNA is identical to that of chimpanzees, our nearest primate relative. Since we grant chimpanzees only limited conscious thinking ability, yet observe that they nonetheless form hierarchical societies with cultural differences, isn't it reasonable to suspect that our basic "human" social behavior also arises from that shared, assumedly unconscious 98 percent? And that it includes what we consider to be our most humane characteristic: an instinct to help and protect tribe members and to not harm them?

Undeniably, we are tribal, territorial animals, and the same programming that causes lesser animals to behave in tribal, territorial ways is also at work in us. The only thing surprising is that we are somehow tricked into believing we're *choosing* to do all the things we do, even when they are instinctive ... programmed. That's why we've been plagued throughout our existence with an inability to understand why we behave as we do. Only in the last decades have neuroscientists uncovered evidence that our brain tricks us into believing our actions are consciously controlled even when they're not. The next chapter, *Deluded Man*, will describe that evidence.

• *Scheduled Development Processes*

Read any book on child development and you will find it dominated with information on the ranges of weeks, months, and years at which particular activities "normally" occur in children. The ages at which babies begin to smile, make eye contact, follow movements, recognize parents, develop hand-eye coordination, crawl, walk, play in particular ways, develop speech, develop "social" skills, etc., are all carefully documented for the doting, concerned new parents. Other books take up where the child-development ones leave off, outlining for teachers, counselors, social workers, and the still-concerned parents the physical, intellectual, moral, and social development to be expected during the years through young adulthood. What is being observed and documented, of course, is the external manifestation of an internal process: the time-and-milestone-correlated development of the brain's wiring – its programming. That is, some wiring cannot occur until a particular window of time during development, and some cannot occur until particular previous wiring has been completed. The process itself is hardwired – preprogrammed – and it in turn firmwires in environment-specific final connections.

The most-documented evidence of this process is in language development – how we learn almost effortlessly to speak whatever languages surround us in early childhood, but later can learn languages only with significant effort. It has been shown convincingly that we come pre-equipped with a language-learning program that functions impressively during the years we're learning to talk ... and then shuts down. Thereafter we must use other, general-purpose learning methods to learn a new language.

An interesting sidelight to this is the phenomena of children – siblings or playmates – occasionally generating a secondary language of their own to converse in quite nicely, thank you, to the bewilderment of everyone else.

Equally interesting is the conjecture that glossolalia – the "speaking in tongues" phenomenon – might arise from our language-learning programming. Although glossolalia is generally associated with charismatic religious circles, it's probable that anyone who wants to and doesn't mind the initial embarrassment can begin speaking aloud in "words," "phrases," and "sentences" not associated with any language. This could be so if the capability arises from a "subprogram" that assists our language-learning programming but doesn't become disabled when the latter does. Who knows?

• *Instinctive Fears*

Once, long ago, Behaviorists ruled the Earth, and it was believed that the only instinct encumbering Man was fear of falling. After all, teams of learned doctors had examined newborn babies, and the only "instinct" they could detect – other than suckling and body functions – was crying and expressions of fear when lowered suddenly as if falling. Consequentially, the prevailing doctrine claimed humans were born as "blank slates" (tabulae rasae) and all our behavior was the result of being "conditioned" by experiences and subsequent feedback. The Behaviorists didn't originate the "tabula rasa" theory – it had an impeccable intellectual pedigree of centuries if not millennia – but they empowered it with the weight of Science and bowled over dissenting voices.

They were wrong, of course.

It has since been determined that few instincts show up in early infancy because our brains are still feverishly wiring and structuring themselves (some say the process continues in diminishing degrees to the early twenties). As described above, many of our instinctive functions are "scheduled" to begin and/or complete at particular times or milestones in the brain's development process. Thus, we don't yet really *know* what fears are instinctive for what periods of time in our development.

Consider fear of the dark. We aren't taught to fear the dark in childhood. In fact, our parents try in vain to teach us to *not* fear it in the safety of our rooms, but nonetheless we develop that fear. Eventually, however, the blanketing irrational fear of the dark fades away and is replaced by specific, rational fears of whatever nighttime predators actually exist. In safe, predator-free neighborhoods – if you're lucky enough to live in one – adults walk the streets and parks at night with no fear. Is instinctive fear of the dark only operable in the period from toddlerhood to young adulthood when we're easy prey for predatory night animals and too inexperienced to avoid them? We don't know.

• *Instinctive Behavior Manifested as Taboos*

Taboos are prohibitions so "sacred" they can't even be discussed; that's their trademark, their definition. Sophisticated societies tend to disparage taboos as being consciously contrived, and the "enlightened" of all generations forever compete to smash "the last taboo" – whatever they deem it to be – and set Mankind free. The spectacle would be endlessly entertaining – like watching puppets in a fiery frenzy to cut their own strings – were it not for the woe their efforts bring upon others. Species-wide taboos exist for a reason, and it's unwise to attempt to override them without first understanding them. "Cures" for conditions not understood are notoriously worse than the conditions. (See Bloodletting.)

Unfortunately there are many *cultural* taboos – pseudo-taboos, if you will – that differ from culture to culture and thus permit drawing the false conclusion that *all* taboos are cultural and perhaps arbitrary. Anthropologists attest, however, that taboos against incest – sexual intercourse between near blood relatives – are present in *all* human cultures, demonstrating they are indeed wired-in: wherever Man is, there they are. Since the potentially dire biological consequence of incest is well known – normally recessive harmful genes can be unleashed – it's generally assumed (probably correctly) that's why the taboo is wired-in, even though we haven't the slightest idea how such an imperative could be encoded in the genes of our DNA and then expanded into behavior-controlling programming in our brains. "Just another miracle of evolution that will be explained someday," we breezily conclude.

Two caveats: One, it's painfully obvious that neither our genetic programming nor its subsequent implementation is 100 percent accurate. ... We still have Siamese twins, horrible genetic diseases, and multitudinous other affronts to our dignity. And two, the incest taboo has sometimes been culturally overridden for the benefit of royal or aristocratic lineages. These two exceptions – when the incest taboo doesn't kick in or is overridden – allow those who'd rather believe Man *isn't* programmed to continue to deny it: some prefer to believe exceptions invalidate a rule rather than prove it.

• *Jung's Archetypal Templates*

Carl G. Jung (1875-1961) invented the concept of human "archetypes" and used it to hypothesize an explanation for the common myths, symbols, and motifs encountered throughout human society. Jung envisioned Man as having a "collective unconscious," a common body of instinctive knowledge containing templates for all the creatures and circumstances likely to be encountered from infancy through old age. The templates – which he called preexisting forms or "archetypes" – became operative when a real-life pattern matching them was encountered, and provided a framework for interpreting and evaluating persons and events. Archetypes for Mother, Father, God, Demons, Heroes, Wise Old Men/Women, etc., were described.

Had knowledge of DNA encoding and computer programming existed earlier, it is very likely Jung would have postulated instead "collective *programming*" containing "*subprograms*" that predispose us to particular behavior at particular times or in particular circumstances. I submit that whether the electrochemical, neurological processes controlling our behavior are described as "programming," "archetypes," or anything else, the reality is the same: We are imposing a hypothetical overlay on observed behavior and guessing how it might be implemented. We have no knowledge at all of how behavior patterns – as opposed to physical characteristics – are encoded in DNA, only the observation that they must be.

• *Gene-based Natures, Talents, Proclivities, Susceptibilities, Etc.*

Few people these days argue that individual "natures" aren't predisposed, but that was very much disputed when the Behaviorists ruled. Their arguments were eventually laid to rest by a now-famous study of identical twins raised in differing environments. The study located and tested adult identical twins separated since infancy by adoption. The similarities of each pair's life choices in vocations, avocations, mates, philosophies, what have you – despite often widely differing environments – were convincing:

They clearly had significant innate programming in common. Not only were their physical abilities – to be athletes, artists, artisans, whatever – wired-in but also their proclivities toward such endeavors, and the attitudes with which they faced the world. The same, of course, is true of *You*. In terms of the age-old debate, yes, you have free will, but nonetheless you are predisposed toward particular roles, actions, and outlooks.

It's serendipitous when our abilities, interests, and attitudes align to make us stellar in some area, for it all depends on the "luck of the roll" of the thirty thousand dice we call genes. It's also the luck of the roll whether we plop into an environment friendly or hostile to our particular drives and talents. As the poet said, "Full many a flower is born to blush unseen," and we flourish or languish, are remembered or forgotten, based on both our innate talents and drives, and our ability to adapt them to our environment.

It should be noted that while genes control our individual traits and dispositions, they can do so only within the range allowed by our species' gene set: each of us has the same closed set of trait-controlling genes (and/or gene combinations), and each gene (or combination) has only a closed set of "choices." While no two humans who aren't identical twins are genetically the same, all of our gene-determined natures must lie within the hardwired limits allowed for human diversity.

When normal, reasonably healthy development in the womb occurs, all humans have the same hardwired programming, regardless of the environment into which they're born. In contrast, our firmwired programming is dependent upon the environment, and effectively creates our interface with it.

Firmwired Human Programming
(Changeable Only With Effort)

• *Behavior Learned Through Scheduled Development Processes*

While the scheduled development programs that enable us to learn necessary and environment-specific skills are hardwired, the programming generated by them to implement the skills usually isn't. If, for example, stroke or trauma damages the speech-programming portion of a brain, it is often possible to relearn to speak; similarly, if a motor-skill-controlling portion is damaged, it is frequently possible to regain use of the affected limbs. Any skill or learning that can be regained – relearned – through therapy is an example of firmwired programming: difficult, but possible.

A caveat: neuroscientists are still studying the brain's "plasticity" – its ability to rewire itself – and differ in their assessments. The safest view at this point seems to be that if sufficient healthy brain tissue remains in the area innately (or developmentally?) dedicated to a particular function, then that function may be relearnable. It is not yet clear to what degree functions can be relearned and wired into portions of the brain not predisposed to them.

• *Surviving and Coping Behavior Learned in Childhood*

When we're conceived, the aforementioned thirty thousand "dice" are tossed, and nine months later we tumble into the world, naked, defenseless, but owners of a vast arsenal of traits determined by that roll of the dice. We're experiments, all of us. Will our particular combination of traits enable us to survive the environment we tumble into? The environment itself is a matter of luck – it may be rich, nurturing, stable, or it may be horrid in a hundred ways. We may survive only seconds, minutes, hours, or we may survive into hoary old age, and whatever period we survive may be mostly satisfying or so miserable we wish we'd never been born.

No matter what our lot or circumstances, from the moment we appear, we begin interacting with our environment with all the skills at our disposal to flatter it into allowing our continued existence. Whatever nature we're blessed or cursed with, we ply it to the task and begin accruing a personal portfolio of survival and coping behavior – a subconscious cataloging of what stratagems worked and what didn't. After the age of our earliest memories, the process becomes gradually less subconscious and more conscious and, concurrently, less firmwired and more softwired.

What evidence is there of this? The evidence lies in the multitude of studies relating the behavior of children raised in dysfunctional families with their subsequent behavior as adults. Studies consistently describe arrays of coping behaviors employed by children and attest to how dismayingly difficult it is to alter those behaviors later in life when they've become inappropriate and harmful. Numerous psychological therapies have been promulgated based on these studies, and in addition to being practiced by psychiatrists, psychologists, and licensed social workers, many have been popularized in self-help books and found their way into self-help groups around the world. The therapies typically involve being led through a painful reexamination and reevaluation of one's childhood environment, discerning the behavior patterns adopted to survive it, and understanding how those patterns now affect adult behavior. Once discerned and understood, the no-longer-appropriate behavior can be modified.

Given the widespread acknowledgment of the strength and persistence of survival and coping behaviors learned in childhood, and the widespread acknowledgment of the considerable effort required to change them, clearly this is prima facie evidence of firmwired programming.

- *Surviving and Coping Behavior Learned With Accompanying Trauma*

War experiences, severe accidents, muggings, rapes, prolonged discrimination, prolonged poverty, unwanted divorces, firings and layoffs, shunning – anything and everything involving physical or emotional trauma can ingrain the behavior adopted to survive it and avoid a repetition. "Once bitten, twice shy," puts it mildly; it's more like, "once traumatized, forever scarred."

The evidence that post-trauma abnormal behavior demonstrates firmwired programming lies – again – in the multitude of studies attempting to understand the observed behavior and in the resulting psychological therapies designed to treat it. Since trauma-induced abnormal behavior can be extreme, treating it is wisely restricted to professional psychologists and psychiatrists rather than allowing self-help groups to jump in. The methods employed, however, differ only in degree: the traumatizing event must be painfully revisited, its reality must be acknowledged and understood, and an attempt must be made to introduce new, more functional coping behavior. In other words, the patient must be reprogrammed.

At some point in human history, the value of deliberately using trauma to reinforce training became noticed, and the military boot camp was born. Everyone who has endured such training can attest to its effectiveness at tearing down ragtag trainees' widely differing images of themselves and building them back up with a common loyalty to their unit and cause.

Unfortunately, more viral examples of deliberate, trauma-induced firmwired programming exist.

"Brainwashing" was brought to the world by the late, unlamented Soviet Communist regime. It deliberately employed prolonged trauma – sleep deprivation accompanied by varying degrees of torture and starvation in a behavioral reward-and-punishment setting – to override existing beliefs with Communist dogma. Similar methods have since been used by some cults to inculcate novices with the cult's beliefs, and parents of young adults in such cults have been known to hire "Deprogrammers" to kidnap their children and subject them to reverse brainwashing.

• *Subconscious Memory*

Subconscious memory may seem like an oxymoron, but it's well proven that we record in memory many things we're not consciously aware of. For example, images viewed by the eye for only milliseconds are recorded by the "subconscious" brain without the "conscious" brain being aware of it. This particular phenomenon, once discovered, became and remains a favored tool in psychological studies. It also achieved notoriety when it was tested by marketers as a means of enhancing the effect of advertisements. That didn't pan out, but it illustrates embarrassingly how quickly anything discovered about human nature is employed to manipulate us for profit.

The existence of subconscious memory actually was theorized by psychoanalytic pioneers long before it was proven. A patient's experience of sudden, unprovoked feelings was often traced to the presence of an object similar to one present at some preceding meaningful or traumatic event; it was conjectured that, although not consciously noticed, the object was unconsciously recorded and associated with the event. Once the patient was made aware of the connection, its effect was diminished or dispelled.

• *Beliefs*

Beliefs are not merely ideas we believe to be true; they are ideas we so strongly believe to be true that somehow they become part of our subconscious behavior-controlling programming. While mere ideas can be debated with a minimum of rancor, beliefs cannot: beliefs, when challenged, trigger a wave of outrage and anger in us, so that we willingly destroy the challengers to whatever degree society and opportunity permits. Once an idea has been promoted to a belief, we no longer control it; instead, it controls us. Thus we willingly die – and kill – for our beliefs. This will be discussed further in Chapter 5, *Idea Man*.

• *Addictive Behavior*

Neuroscientists caution us that brain processes are complex, interwoven, and nowhere close to being fully understood. As a consequence, most descriptions of how the brain "works" are simplifications incorporating what is known about a primary process, ignoring interactions with secondary processes, and glossing over the still unknown details.

With that caveat in mind, it is generally accepted as established that addictive behavior is the result of a "chemical imbalance" in the brain. The imbalance most often is in the level of dopamine, a neurotransmitter associated with feelings of pleasure, elation, and euphoria. Dopamine also appears to have a role in imprinting – programming – behaviors that lead to a spurt in the level of dopamine. All the things that naturally bring us pleasure – eating chocolate, enjoying music, receiving praise, winning a gamble, enjoying sex – have been found to raise the level of dopamine. Presumably, the greater the pleasure the greater the associated rise in dopamine.

It is also known that our preferred addictive drugs –
alcohol, nicotine, marijuana, amphetamines, cocaine,
heroin – artificially raise the level of dopamine by either
increasing its rate of release or slowing its rate of
reabsorption. When the artificial "high" is strong enough or
repeated enough, the brain effectively short-circuits and
reprograms itself to repeat the actions that led to the
euphoria: this is *not* a conscious decision to repeat a
pleasant experience; it's an unconscious, firmwired craving
that causes desperation and physiological symptoms when
denied.

To make addiction even crueler, Mother Nature doesn't
appreciate being tampered with and reacts to repeated,
artificially high jolts of dopamine by decreasing the level of
dopamine produced normally. So addicts end up having to
take drugs, not to experience euphoria, but to simply stop
feeling miserable and feel "normal." Attempting to regain
the lost euphoria can lead to stronger drugs, higher
dosages ... and often to overdoses and death.

• *Ingrained Habits*

Habits straddle the border between firmwired and
softwired programming. They're the things we do so often
we can do them unconsciously – or in dictionary terms,
"recurrent patterns of behavior acquired through frequent
repetition, often done without conscious thought." This
covers a wide range of behaviors, from activities performed
at particular times to mannerisms employed in particular
circumstances. Some habits are more "unconscious" than
others, however. If we are interrupted and questioned
about our behavior, we will unabashedly admit to some
things being habits, but will bewilderedly wonder what's
being talked about in the case of others. Some habits, it
seems, we are aware of, and others we are not. The habits
we aren't aware of are the ones that are "firmwired" and

devilishly difficult to change or break. The more easily changed habits reside in our softwired programming, because to be readily changeable we must be aware of them; they must be consciously accessible.

Softwired Human Programming (Changeable)

• *Superficial Habits*

These are habits we are aware of, readily admit, and can modify fairly easily – as opposed to the firmwired "ingrained habits" described previously.

• *Knowledge Gained Through Observation and Experience*

Everything we consciously observe and experience throughout our lives becomes part of a personal database from which we constantly distill knowledge – rules for surviving and placating our environment, ideas for enhancing our existence.

• *Knowledge Gained Through Being Taught*

Much of our knowledge comes from being explicitly taught rather than by chance learning. Modern societies accumulate so much knowledge that childhood and adolescence are devoted almost entirely to being taught the things deemed necessary to be a useful citizen. Those having the requisite ability, interest, and opportunity continue to be taught into adulthood, some until they have mastered all that is presently known in a particular discipline and are ready to begin extending that knowledge.

• *Knowledge Deduced or Extrapolated From Existing Knowledge*

Wherever we stop along the path of formal education, if we have adequately learned the skills of reading, writing, and critical thinking, we can and do continue to learn on our own. Whatever we read or experience, we are always comparing it with our present knowledge, evaluating it, and deriving new knowledge.

· · ·

This completes the overview of our human programming. I trust you observed that when we got to softwired programming – that over which we exert control – the catalog rapidly dwindled away into forms of "knowledge." That knowledge, however, includes everything we proudly see as defining humanity: our literature, art, and architecture, our music, math, and medicines, our sciences, philosophies, and religions … all arising somehow from that mere two-or-whatever percent of DNA that differentiates us from chimpanzees. We nervously ask: Are our vaunted intellectual achievements merely superficial, softwired distractions that entertain us while our hardwired traits and firmwired beliefs drive us to continual warfare? Are the wondrous abilities and accomplishments that make us forget we're animals just things we fiddle with while burning Rome … or Dresden … or Hiroshima?

Alas! Mankind, the eternal contradiction, stands with branches straining skyward and roots mired in mud; our lifetimes and generations are spent trying vainly to reconcile lofty ideas with base actions; we are like riders on a wild beast over which we have but marginal control, forever attempting to explain and justify the beast's behavior. Only when we finally come to understand the hidden programming controlling our behavior will there be any hope for change.

And standing in the way, of course, is our absolute conviction that we are *consciously deciding* what we do rather than responding to unconscious programming.

While we're willing to admit that our "automatic" functions and a few other things are programmed, we balk at the claim that our *behavior* is programmed because we *know* that we are constantly consciously deciding what we do.

Are we?

Or is it just an illusion created by our brain?

Can our brain *trick* us into believing our actions are consciously controlled even when they're not? The next chapter, *Deluded Man*, presents evidence this is so.

Chapter 2
Deluded Man:
The Illusion of Conscious Control

"We all do no end of feeling, and we mistake it for thinking." – Mark Twain

The radical notion that "We are not in conscious control of much of our behavior, but are deluded by our brains into believing that we are" is not a notion to be proffered lightly: it's unsettling, unflattering, and ... frankly, frightening. It's the sort of notion to be considered only as a last resort, when confronted with undeniable evidence. Such evidence accrued slowly, but by 1985 had become sufficient. That's when Dr. Michael S. Gazzaniga, a leading neuroscientist in the assault on the brain's secrets, wrote *The Social Brain: Discovering the Networks of the Mind.*

In that seminal book for nonscientists, he laid out clearly the accumulating evidence that brain mechanisms do indeed delude us into believing we consciously decide to do things that are actually decided unconsciously. He dubbed the brain function primarily responsible for this delusion the "interpreter."

In 1998 Dr. Gazzaniga followed up with another book, *The Mind's Past*, which once again emphasized the significance of the interpreter function, documented the now greater evidence of its existence, and philosophized on its role in the "mind." Both of these books are extremely readable and very thorough; they provide all the notes, citations, and references dear to academia, and make a powerful case for the existence of an interpreter function in the brain.

That this important concept *still* hasn't become mainstream reflects a corollary: our internal programming is so potent that we routinely – and unconcernedly – discard data conflicting with existing beliefs. Nonetheless, the accumulating evidence supporting the existence of the interpreter function (which I prefer to call the "Great Explainer") can't be ignored forever, so let me try to convince *You* with a summary of some of the evidence gleaned from those books.

• • •

Workmen are no better than their tools. And the tools available for studying the brain have improved dramatically over the last half century: better methods for staining tissue to trace neural circuitry; new technologies for real-time observation of the portions of the brain working on a problem; refined techniques for detecting and sending signals to individual brain cells via electrodes and measuring the time between events; new methods for investigating the complex microbiology going on at the synapses; improved gadgetry for sending visual stimuli selectively to the two hemispheres of the brain – all of these enable the hardworking, ever-curious neuroscientists to acquire hard data to make, break, and remake their theories and speculations on how the brain works its magic.

One of the early clues that something strange was going on in the brain was the discovery that brain circuits that become active when a particular motor action – movement – is about to take place do so *before* the brain circuits that become active when that action is consciously perceived. Peculiar. Here we have portions of the brain wherein lies our consciousness, and portions wherein lies our unconscious muscle control circuitry, and the latter become active before the former when an action takes place. Yet we *know* that the opposite is true: we consciously decide to move, and then we move. If ever anything cried out to be more thoroughly investigated, this was it. And it was ... thoroughly.

Eking out the truths took years of ingenious, painstaking experiments and, I suspect, some attitude adjustment. It's one thing to admit in the abstract that "All we experience is what the brain allows us to experience" and quite another to encounter that truth in action. It's as if one "believed" in angels and demons, but then one day began actually *seeing* them. A world of difference, and by their own admission the experimenters didn't like it any better than we do. Nonetheless, the results are in, and they are incontestable ... or at least they would be were we rational and honest rather than swayed by beliefs and feelings.

Signals moving along neural pathways take time, just as do signals moving through electrical wire, but signals moving from one portion of the brain to another have been observed to take additional time, apparently depending upon the amount of processing going on in transit. It has been determined that it takes only about two-hundredths of a second for a sensory signal to travel from the skin to the sensory area of the cortex, but about *half a second* more for the signal to show up in the conscious area of the cortex. Thus, whether an experimenter delivers a pulse directly to your skin or simulates it by sending a pulse to the sensory area of your cortex, it still takes up to half a second after that for you to become conscious of it.

This clearly isn't good for survival, so the brain doesn't wait around for conscious awareness; as soon as a signal hits the sensory cortex it becomes available to invoke unconscious, automatic programming to respond to it. No wonder we're startled when our arm suddenly jerks back when our fingers encounter something hot or sharp; it happens half a second before our conscious mind is aware there's a problem.

So far, so good. None of this disturbs us ... until the experimenters inform us that the phenomenon of motor cortex activity occurring before conscious awareness activity also occurs for "consciously decided" movements, such as picking up a pencil, taking off our glasses, or turning this page: the motor control neurons can be seen kicking in before the conscious awareness neurons, even though we perceive the opposite to be true.

To investigate why, experimenters worked with patients whose medical treatment required the placement of electrodes in their brains and who were willing to participate in neurological tests. It was found that if a stimulus is given directly to the sensory cortex and a second stimulus is given to the skin up to half a second later, the patient will report, and insist, that the second stimulus came before the first. This shouldn't be. Even if the two stimuli were given simultaneously, it would still take the skin stimulus two-hundredths of a second to reach the sensory cortex, so how could the patient possibly experience the second stimulus before the first?

A hypothesis was made that the conscious brain somehow "refers" its awareness of a skin stimulus back to when the sensory cortex received it, mere hundredths of a second after the skin was touched, rather than to when the conscious brain received it half a second later; it was further hypothesized that a stimulus given directly to the sensory cortex provides no such reference, so the conscious brain has to treat it as if it had occurred when the signal reached it, half a second after its actual occurrence.

To test the hypothesis, the experiment was altered so that the first stimulus, instead of being applied to the sensory cortex, was applied to a neural pathway leading from the midbrain to the sensory cortex, a pathway that was known to generate a quick-arriving signal similar to the skin's. This time the patients reported receiving the signals in the correct sequence because now *both* became time-referenced back to when the sensory cortex received the signals rather than when the conscious brain received them. The hypothesis was thus verified: our conscious awareness *is* up to half a second behind our sensory input and, unknown to us, the brain makes temporal corrections based on when the sensory cortex receives the signals so that we *think* we're conscious of them as they occur. The dismaying reality is not only that "All we can experience is what the brain allows us to experience," but that we can experience it only as occurring at the time the brain tells us it occurred.

The brain's temporal trick of backdating awareness is but one of the stratagems it uses to delude us. Another is its penchant for distributing input data to a slew of specialized processing modules, then assembling and analyzing the results to generate a single, consistent interpretation of the data ... even if it has to fudge the results a little.

One of the most thoroughly studied and documented demonstrations of this is in the brain's handling of visual data. It was once thought, reasonably, that light impinging upon the rods and cones of the eye's retina generated signals that were carried via the optic nerve to the brain's visual cortex where the image was essentially reproduced and interpreted. Well, the beginning and end were somewhat correct – the retina does generate signals, most of which eventually reach the visual cortex, and the visual cortex does play a major role in interpreting them – but what goes on before and after is wilder and woollier than expected.

Processing actually begins in the retina itself: we're now told it has twelve layers of specialized cells that "talk" with one another through neuronal connections to glean and refine particular information, such as color, edges, contours, uniform areas, movement, etc. What gets passed to the primary visual cortex is not a simple overall image of what is being viewed, but multiple, separate, continuously changing mappings of the features being detected. Dedicated areas of the primary visual cortex further process these mappings and generate two streams of visual data that go to separate regions of the neocortex for yet more processing; the two streams are sometimes called the "where" and "what" streams since one specializes in detecting where things are and the other specializes in identifying what things are. Somewhere, somehow, in some way, the output of all these processing modules is miraculously combined to produce our conscious perception of continuous, seamless, three-dimensional, full-color, all-encompassing vision – something that actually exists nowhere except as the end product.

It's an amazing system.

That the brain processes vision modularly was hypothesized long before improved technology and painstaking research could prove it, for it had long been observed that lesions in particular portions of the brain interfered with some aspects of vision but didn't affect others. Similarly, it had been long hypothesized that when visual data is incomplete or conflicting, the brain might "fill in the blanks" to generate a holistic picture, for it had long been observed that optical illusions occur consistently in particular circumstances.

That hypothesis, too, has been validated: rather than present an incomplete or ambiguous picture, our brain will make up the most plausible (to it) solution and render it to us as reality – thereby creating optical illusions. Examples of optical illusions you're probably familiar with include: the two-dimensional line drawings that flip-flop between two possible interpretations, the "impossible architecture" of M.C. Escher, the identical parallelograms that appear different sizes if depicted as rectangular tabletops being viewed from the side or the end, the circle of slanted lines that appears to rotate when the circle's distance from the eye is varied back and forth. All of these illusions occur because the brain is making up a plausible explanation for the disparate input it's receiving and presenting it as reality. Keep this in mind as we now consider some of the most mind-boggling behavior ever documented in Man.

• • •

It all began with the study of "split-brain" epileptic patients in the 1960s. Epilepsy is a devastating disease – abnormal electrical discharges beginning at one or more locations in the brain can spread throughout, resulting in convulsions and unconsciousness. It is treated primarily with anticonvulsant medication, secondarily with surgery to remove the tissue where the discharges start, and as a last resort with split-brain surgery to separate the two hemispheres of the brain and prevent the discharges from spreading from one half of the brain to the other.

Amazingly, and fortunately, the split-brain surgery not only reduces the epilepsy to a level treatable with medicine, but the patients appear otherwise unaffected by it. This, of course, intrigued neuroscientists, so they sought and got permission from patients to test their abilities both before surgery and in the years following surgery. Never was Pandora's Box opened so innocently.

It was already known at the time that the two hemispheres of our brain, now often referred to as our "left brain" and "right brain," split the responsibility of monitoring and controlling the two halves of our body equally: all sensory input – sight, hearing, and touch – from the left side of our body is transmitted to the right brain, and all sensory input from the right side of our body is transmitted to the left brain; similarly, the left brain controls all of the voluntary muscle movement on the right side of our body, and the right brain controls all on the left. This, of course, is why brain damage from a stroke or trauma affects abilities on the opposite side of the body.

Speech, however, is different: it isn't divided between the two hemispheres. With rare exceptions, the ability to speak and to process language resides in only one hemisphere, and for about 93 percent of us it's in the left hemisphere. Because of this preponderance – and to avoid the annoyance of having to continually qualify statements – it's become customary to talk and write as if language is always in the left brain. I will do this, too, because the important thing – the only significant thing – is that speech processing exists in only *one* hemisphere and not in the other. Yes, strange as it sounds, only one of our two half-brains has the ability to speak what it knows, and the other does not. On the rare occasions that speech processing ability is found in both hemispheres, it is fully developed in only one and is very limited in the other.

Thus our abilities to process language and to speak are affected by stroke or trauma only when damage occurs in particular areas of the "speaking" brain.

These circumstances – that only one of our two half-brains can speak and that each of them can directly sense and control only half of our body – obviously pose no problems for us, since we're serenely unaware of them and routinely function as though we had a single fully integrated brain. And that's because we actually do, thanks to some remarkable communication "cables" that intimately connect the two hemispheres and enable each to know everything the other is experiencing and doing all the time. Both half-brains consequently have access to the language-processing and speaking areas of the left brain, so both are able to speak what they know.

The largest of the communication paths is one that is clearly visible in most pictures and sketches of the brain, for it looks much like a computer ribbon cable connecting the two halves. It's about the thickness and width of your palm and has the magnificent name "corpus callosum." It contains an estimated two hundred million nerve fibers, each transmitting an average of twenty signals a second. That's four billion signals a second communicating back and forth constantly. High-level information, like vision, hearing, and sensory input, is transmitted between the two hemispheres across this path, and it's this path that must be severed to allow patients with severe epilepsy to survive.

Once a patient has his corpus callosum severed – "splitting" the two halves of his brain and preventing epileptic seizures from spreading to the other half – only his left brain will now have access to the language-processing and speaking functions, so now only his left brain will be able to speak. The patient will be able to answer questions only about things that are known by his left brain. This startling reality proved to be a dominant phenomenon throughout post-operative testing: patients could verbally report on information present in their left hemispheres, but not on information present in their right hemispheres.

In order to provide information selectively to one hemisphere or the other during testing, use was made of the fact that wherever we look, everything to the left of the point we're focusing on is sent to the right brain and everything to the right is sent to the left brain. Thus, if we're gazing fixedly at the center of a projection screen and something is displayed to the left of center, it will be transmitted to the right brain, and if something is displayed to the right of center, it will be transmitted to the left brain. Normally whatever is seen by one hemisphere is immediately passed to the other across the corpus callosum bridge, but in split-brain patients this can't occur, so differing information can be presented to each hemisphere. Because our eyes tend to dart around even when we try to hold them fixed, the information is flashed on the screen for so brief a time that it can be consciously recognized but then disappears before the eyes can shift and allow the other hemisphere to see it too.

Imagine, then, the following test scenarios:

A split-brain patient sits at a testing table in front of a projection screen; while the patient focuses on a small mark at the center of the screen, a symbol is flashed to the left or the right half of the screen and the patient asked to identify it. Before the operation the patient could readily name the symbols flashed to either side; now, after the operation, he as readily names the symbols flashed on the right side (to his left, speaking brain) but claims to see nothing except maybe a flash of light when they're flashed on the left side (to his right, nonspeaking brain).

The operation changed nothing affecting the transmittal of images from his eyes to his brain: the left-side images assumedly still arrive in the right brain, and they assumedly are still processed by it, but then they come to a dead end at the severed corpus callosum. Nothing passes to the left, speaking brain, so it gains no knowledge; when asked what it saw, it replies honestly, "I saw nothing." Its silent partner, the nonspeaking brain, undoubtedly hears all this – since the left ear's transmitting auditory signals to it – and knows very well what it saw, but can't say so!

To test this, a row of cards having pictures of the various symbols being flashed is placed in front of the patient, and he is asked to point, sometimes with his left hand, sometimes with his right, to the card containing the symbol that has just been flashed. Sure enough, when a symbol is flashed to his right brain, even though his left brain vehemently denies having seen anything and his right hand (controlled by the left brain) can't point to correct cards with more than chance accuracy, his left hand (controlled by the right brain) unerringly and effortlessly picks the correct card every time.

In a modification of the test, pictures of variously shaped solid objects are flashed on the screen and a covered tray containing a collection of the objects is placed in front of the patient. After an object is flashed, the patient is asked to feel in the tray for that object. Again, the patient denies having seen anything flashed to the right brain, but unerringly selects the object from the tray with his left hand while doing so only at a chance level with his right hand.

These early tests with split-brain patients were powerful and intriguing. Naturally, neuroscientists wanted to find out more: did the hemispheres' abilities differ in other ways besides language, or did they otherwise share tasks and abilities equally?

To compare the two hemispheres' power of inference, two pictures were flashed simultaneously, one to each hemisphere, and the patient was instructed to use both hands to pick which two of a series of cards in front of him contained pictures that were *related* to the two flashed. In one example, as described in Dr. Gazzaniga's books, a picture of a chicken claw was flashed to the left brain and a picture of a snow scene was flashed to the right brain; the patient selected a picture of a chicken with his right hand, to match the picture of the chicken claw, and selected a picture of a snow shovel with his left hand, to match the picture of the snow scene. When asked why he'd chosen those two, his left, speaking brain answered easily and quickly, "Why the chicken goes with the chicken claw and the shovel's needed to clean out the chicken shed." Although the left brain knew nothing of the snow scene and hadn't a clue why the left hand chose the shovel, it instantly and effortlessly made up a reason ... and believed it.

Thus began the revealing of the "Great Explainer."

As testing of additional patients proceeded, it was found that a few had limited language ability in their right brains in addition to the full language capability in their left: while they couldn't speak from the right brain or employ rules of grammar, they could recognize and comprehend most nouns and verbs. This allowed the mute right brain to become more active during testing. The word "smile" could be flashed to the right brain, and the patient would smile; if asked why, he would calmly provide a reason: "I just thought it funny you always wear a bow tie." The word "walk" could be flashed, and the patient would get up and begin walking away; if asked why, he would calmly explain he was going to get a drink, a coke, to stretch his legs, or whatever. *Never* would the Great Explainer in the left brain be nonplused nor seem surprised by whatever action the right brain initiated, but would calmly explain it away with varying degrees of logic.

It soon became apparent that whenever the nonspeaking hemisphere caused the performance of some action unbeknownst to the speaking hemisphere, the speaking hemisphere would immediately generate some explanation for it – sometimes plausible, sometimes outrageous – to make the action seem deliberate. What's more, the subject would truly believe the explanation and defend it, angrily if necessary: "I *told* you, I just wanted to stretch my legs!" This in spite of the fact the patients frequently were highly intelligent people, fully aware of the nature of the tests, and capable of saying, "I don't know why I did what I did, it must have been my right brain responding to some instruction you gave it." But they didn't say that. They didn't say it because they thought they *did* know why they did it. They thought – and totally believed – the unconsciously generated explanation actually *was* the reason for their action, that they had consciously decided it. The self-generated explanations were so strongly convincing that they were never suspect, despite the circumstances, and despite sometimes being glaringly illogical. The Great Explainer in our brain is totally convincing, and is never questioned.

• • •

So, after these many millennia, we've finally begun – just begun – to acquire useful information to apply to our eternal, anguished lament, "Why do we war rather than live in peace?" Were we simply animals rather than thinking people there'd be no puzzlement over our behavior – why *shouldn't* we be like other territorial colonies, packs, and tribes, and regard alien groups of our own species as rivals to be overcome or destroyed? It's only because we're convinced by our brains that everything we do is by conscious choice rather than unconscious instinct that we're continually amazed and appalled that our behavior is typical of tribal, territorial animals. Once we realize and accept that much of our behavior actually *is* controlled by instincts – subconscious programming – and that the brain's Great Explainer function *deludes* us into believing that whatever we do was consciously decided upon for a reason, *then* we can get on with finding ways to cope with our hidden programming ... and perhaps live in peace.

• • •

But first we need to examine one more way our brain deludes us.

The next chapter, *Biased Man*, examines the "bias" phenomenon and its role in "polarization." Bias and polarization have often been commented upon but have never been adequately explained. Until now.

Chapter 3
Biased Man: The Illusion of Impartiality

"This rule is perfect: in all matters of opinion our adversaries are insane. ... Where prejudice exists it always discolors our thoughts." – Mark Twain

Why is it we can discuss most ideas rationally, but other ideas inevitably provoke great passion and little rationality? What within us causes this dichotomy between ordinary ideas and "fighting" ideas?

We're told that frogs that catch insects on the fly using long whip-like tongues have an interesting limitation: only insects of a particular size flying by are considered food. If someone with the innocent curiosity of a small boy tears wings from the frog's favorite insects before dumping them in his terrarium, the frog may starve to death while the live, edible bugs crawl all over him; he's programmed to recognize only flying insects as prey, and the crawling insects are no more considered a food source than are pebbles, twigs, and small boys. Could we, somehow, be similarly programmed to accept only ideas meeting particular subconscious criteria, and to blindly reject others?

What if, for example, before an idea is processed by our conscious brain, it is subjected to a hierarchy of tests in our subconscious brain and tagged with an appropriate level of "for" or "against" emotion to indicate how strongly it should be accepted or rejected? The tests might include whether the idea was introduced by a friend or foe, and how well the idea aligned with our existing beliefs and disbeliefs: Is it a great truth fully in accord with our present understanding and expanding upon it? Is it a mere restatement of what we already believe? Is it a partial truth, in accord with some of our beliefs but opposing others? Is it neutral, neither confirming nor threatening any of our present beliefs, and therefore safe to be treated with intellectual fairness? Is it a falsehood containing perhaps a grain of truth but denying or distorting other things we know to be true? Is it an outright lie, obviously emanating from the other side? The emotion generated by the answers to the unconscious tests could then cue us, and the Great Explainer, to respond to the idea accordingly.

"Well," you say, "this example is only a hypothetical what-if and doesn't merit serious consideration." Regretfully, I must inform you that nearly *all* of our traditional theories about how our brain/mind works by our most learned doctors and scientists are also only what-ifs and as-ifs. From Freud, Jung, Adler, et al. on down, we've been essentially reaching blindfolded into a gunny sack in a dark room with thick socks over our hands and trying to describe whatever our grope encounters. All of the images, entities, and nomenclature we've come up with while trying to identify and "explain" the phenomena we've encountered have been as-ifs and what-ifs. Id, ego, libido, complexes, repression, introversion, extroversion, persona, anima/animus, the inner child, etc., all are made-up theories attempting to explain observed phenomena by saying, "It's as if."

Consider Dr. Carl G. Jung's concept of "complexes." It arose from word-association tests during which Jung would speak a word to a patient, and the patient would respond with the first word that came to mind. Jung observed that for some words there was a noticeable delay before the patient responded and that the patient was unable to explain the delay and was often unaware of it. To investigate, Jung began including psychologically related words in the tests and carefully timing the intervals between test words and responses. Based on the results, he hypothesized that it was *as if* there were associated clusters (complexes) of feelings, thoughts, and memories in the unconscious, and that any word touching upon the complex would cause a delayed response. Eventually he came to see the complexes *as if* they were autonomous fiefdoms within the personality, capable of influencing thoughts and behavior.

Knowing what we now know, we can reinterpret Jung's data to describe not "complexes," but rather complex, time-absorbing parallel processing going on to resolve the competing, sometimes conflicting ideas evoked by the words. The extensive research on how the brain processes visual data, reviewed in the last chapter, demonstrates beyond doubt that the brain can and does use modular parallel processing, and can and does meld the output of many modules to achieve a unified result. Thus it is not unreasonable to view Dr. Jung's data as demonstrating similar unconscious processing of ideas.

What about the emotional content associated with some ideas?

Brain research has shown that the brain can and does generate emotional signals to communicate "feelings."

Suspicion that this was so began during tests with split-brain patients, when mischievous neuroscientists occasionally flashed a nude pinup to the nonspeaking hemisphere, and the patients often evidenced amusement or embarrassment without knowing why. They'd blame either "that machine" or the neuroscientist. This showed that even though their speaking hemisphere couldn't receive visual data across the severed corpus callosum, the speaking brain was clearly receiving some form of emotional signals through other neural pathways. It also revealed that the Great Explainer function explains away unexpected feelings as easily as unexpected actions. As usual, the neuroscientists proceeded to devise tests to eke out more information.

In one test, patients were asked to rate how much they liked or disliked particular words, such as *mom, war, algebra, home, TV,* etc. To establish what the right hemisphere thought of the words emotionally, the words were flashed to the right brain and the patient told to use his left hand to point to a number on a scale to rate them. With this established, the words were then flashed a second time to the right brain, and the patient told to *speak* a number of the scale to rate them. Since the left, speaking brain didn't know what the words were, it had to rely on whatever "like" or "dislike" feeling it sensed to announce a rating. Nonetheless, the ratings sensed and spoken by the left brain closely tracked the ratings pointed to by the right brain: emotional cues were being passed from one hemisphere to the other through neural pathways other than those that had been severed.

In another test, a sophisticated gadget that could present short mood-evoking film clips exclusively to the right brain was used. After viewing a clip and being asked how they felt, the patients could accurately report via their left brain whatever feeling, from scared to pleasant, had been evoked in the right brain. Although the "language" of the brain's emotional messaging is unknown, and our attempts to verbalize feelings are coarse and clumsy, there's little doubt that nuanced emotional messages are indeed passed from one hemisphere to the other through "lower" neural pathways.

This knowledge makes possible the following hypothesis: the brain processes an idea by presenting it in parallel to arrays of modules that evaluate it using differing criteria; the results are melded to generate an emotional cue that reflects the merit of the idea; the Great Explainer uses the cue to generate appropriate pro or con arguments.

If this hypothesis is correct, it is probable that our emotional response to an idea doesn't stem from our rational evaluation of the idea, but rather that our "rational" assessment of an idea is the result of the Great Explainer justifying an emotionally tagged "best match" of how well it conforms to our beliefs and interests. Thus we respond to ideas impugning existing beliefs irrationally, emotionally, and inevitably in the way most favorable to us. We – all of us – are inherently biased; it's neither a liberal phenomenon nor a conservative phenomenon, but a human phenomenon.

This subconscious processing is clearly sophisticated and cunning. It doesn't fall into the trap of approving ideas that agree with our *professed* beliefs when the end result would be unfavorable to us. A "foolish consistency" is not the hobgoblin of our unconscious mind. Were we polled concerning our beliefs on a number of basic issues and a computer program employing pure unweighted logic used to predict our responses to related issues, the program would fail miserably. It would imagine that people who professed caring about a strong national defense would favor investigating and eliminating waste and corruption from the military-industrial complex, and that people who professed caring about the needy would favor investigating and eliminating waste and corruption from the social-welfare system.

The reality is that the opposite is true.

No, the bottom line for our unconscious evaluation of ideas is not achieving logical consistency, but defending our existing beliefs. As soon as our unconscious processing determines that an opponent is attempting to discredit or dismember "our" ideas or "our" programs, we automatically and angrily deny any flaws that could provide them an opportunity.

This leads in to another phenomenon – polarization.

Wherever we turn we find ourselves divided into opposing camps that differ diametrically on the positions taken on a wide range of subjects. Whenever an opinion expressed by one camp is challenged by the opposing camp, the "opinions" quickly migrate toward the extremes and become tenets to be defended to the death. Whenever any new idea is proposed that might however tenuously sway the argument one way or the other, it is immediately and vehemently embraced or rejected by members of the camps based solely upon their biases – whether it could be used to strengthen or weaken their positions. Rationality and reasonableness are not factors, let alone consistency or truthfulness.

Consider the following list of late twentieth-century subjects that became polarized: while these viscerally debatable subjects appear at first to be simple "pro or con" issues – making "black or white" reactions reasonable – closer consideration reveals that forming an opinion on any one of them requires integrating opinions on numerous underlying issues, most of which are also two-sided.

Women's Rights for Abortion	*Babies Rights to Life*
Civil Rights	*Civil Obedience*
Affirmative Action	*Racial Quotas*
Separation of Church and State	*Freedom of Religion*
Gun Control	*Right to Bear Arms*
The National Education Assoc.	*The National Rifle Assoc.*
Bilingual Public Schools	*English as Official Language*
Free Speech	*Pornography*
Open Marriages	*Legislation of Morality*
Welfare Programs	*Military Spending*
The ACLU	*The CIA*
Big Labor	*Big Business*
Socialism	*Capitalism*
Gay Marriage	*Gay Bashing*
Capital Punishment	*Coddling of Criminals*
The Vietnam War	*Peaceniks*
The Draft	*Draft Dodgers*
et cetera	*ad nauseam*

For example, your opinion on abortion will undoubtedly be affected by your opinions on:

- Does unrestricted abortion promote unrestricted sexual freedom?
- Is unrestricted sexual freedom good or bad?
- Does unrestricted sexual freedom result in the breakdown of "traditional" families?
- Are "traditional" families essential to human society, or are they simply one of many viable alternatives?

• • •

- Is taking human life permissible under any circumstances?
- What circumstances?
- Is a first-trimester fetus a "human life"?

· Do any/many/most unwanted babies subsequently have lives such that they wish they'd never been born?
· Are any/many/most unwanted babies subsequently adopted into an environment that allows a meaningful life?

• • •

· Do individuals have rights relative to society?
· Does society have rights relative to individuals?
· Do individuals have responsibilities to society?
· Does society have responsibilities to individuals?
· What are the rights and responsibilities of individuals?
· What are the rights and responsibilities of society?

• • •

· Is there a God?
· If there is a God, are there God-ordained laws that must be followed?
· If there are God-ordained laws, are they absolute and inflexible or relative to human circumstances?

• • •

· Can morality be legislated?
· Should morality be legislated?
· Who decides what is moral?

Logic suggests that opinions dependent upon a large number of underlying issues should result in a continuum of opinions (and emotional involvement) between two possible extremes – in this case between unrestricted abortion and banned abortion. If the underlying factors were mutually independent and sufficient in number, we might even expect the familiar bell-shaped curve of a "normal distribution" between the two extremes. Instead we repeatedly encounter the polarization phenomenon – opinions coalesced to two mutually blind and unyielding positions close to the extremes rather than the middle: we end up either in a group blindly demanding unrestricted abortion for any reason whatsoever or in a group blindly demanding banning all abortions whatsoever.

While most divisive issues admittedly haven't sufficient independent underlying factors to expect a normal distribution, there surely are sufficient "only slightly dependent" factors to reasonably expect something other than the polarization actually observed. And what about the emotional extremism? Theoretically, the issues and underlying factors could be discussed with a minimum of emotional involvement, but reality proves otherwise. Clearly the polarization phenomenon is neither reasoned nor rational ... a sure sign of instincts – programming – at work.

Consider this: If we believe in "Liberalism," we dismiss conservative thought as an oxymoron; if we believe in "Conservatism," we reject liberal thought as destructive of society; if we believe in "God," it's a mark of faith to disdain the false teachings of the Godless; if we believe in "no-God," it's a mark of intelligence to disdain the incendiary superstitions of the Believers. It is seldom and with extreme reluctance that we ever admit that an idea from an opposing camp might have merit.

To observe this phenomenon repeatedly and still imagine it to be the product of rational thought is in itself an impressive tribute to our powers of self-deception – no, self-blindness. This tendency is one of the most glaringly obvious characteristics of our species, yet to us it's nearly invisible. Even when an issue divides us right down the middle and some seer points out how unlikely it is that there's a "right" and a "wrong" side – "Surely half our population can't be totally wrong, thoughtless, or uncaring; there must be some valid basis for both viewpoints" – even though we agree with this abstraction, nod our heads, and make appropriate noises, we go right on as before: "We" are right and good; "They" are wrong and evil.

We do not rationally choose to persist in blind, one-sided views of those things that stir us to anger: we are compelled to do so, programmed to do so. Even when confronted with the reality that some of those taking the opposing viewpoint are people we know to be conscientious, caring persons, we can only express dismay, hurt, and bewilderment that they can be so wrong on this issue, so blind to the truth. It simply never occurs to us, or them, that both views may be "right," that both positions may stem from valid concerns for human well-being, but that differing natures and experiences cause us to fear different dangers. Just as when driving down a road we can veer into a ditch to either the left or the right, in human affairs there's almost always two ways to go wrong.

Proverbs and folk sayings of all lands reflect this dualism: We say, "Look before you leap," but also that "He who hesitates is lost." We say, "Nothing ventured, nothing gained," but also that "A bird in the hand's worth two in the bush." If someone or some society is drifting toward danger on the left, the proper advice is "turn right," but if they're drifting toward danger on the right, the proper advice is, "turn left." Somehow, sadly, we seem to be wired to recognize only one danger at a time, either the ditch to the left or the ditch to the right, but not both. If someone warns of danger in the direction we're careening, we think they're mad, delusional, and wanting to drive us into the ditch we're avoiding – ergo, they must be evil.

I do not know, you do not know, and the learned doctors do not know how our brain functions to achieve the results it does. The facts that are known are meager compared to the theories we generate from them. We understand even less about how the brain becomes "the mind." Nonetheless, the evidence is overwhelming that something in the way our brains function causes us to be biased – to respond to ideas impinging upon existing beliefs irrationally, emotionally, and inevitably in whatever way is most favorable to us. Further, whenever our beliefs are opposed, our biases drive us to become polarized – to migrate to an extreme position.

• • •

We now have sufficient background information – three chapters' worth – to begin examining our species programming. The next chapter, *Tribal Man*, will describe the overarching tribal, territorial-animal programming that defines our species and controls our behavior.

Chapter 4
Tribal Man: The Tribal Template Controlling Human Behavior

"I am the entire human race compacted together. I have found that there is no ingredient of the race which I do not possess in either a large way or a small way."
– Mark Twain

If you imagine that "tribal" is descriptive only of primitive societies, think again. We demonstrate tribal behavior every hour of our waking life, even when we're blissfully unaware of it – *especially* when we're unaware of it – and the tenets of the tribes we belong to continuously mold, direct, and limit our thinking and behavior.

"What tribes?" you may ask. All of them: your family tribe, your social-circle and workplace tribes, your religious and political tribes, your national tribe ... all of them. If you believe these are not tribes, that they're simply people you associate with, and who certainly don't control your thinking any more than you control theirs, I say, "We shall see."

For millennia we didn't think of ourselves as animals, but nonetheless we were. When the evidence finally forced us to admit maybe we are animals, we hastily added, "but *special* animals, ones not controlled by instinct." That indulgence isn't weathering well, either: Chapter 1, *Programmed Man*, cataloged some of the instincts now acknowledged to exist, and Chapters 2 and 3, *Delusional Man* and *Biased Man*, gave warning that as the concealing curtain of the Great Explainer function is lifted, much more of our behavior will be recognized as instinctive – programmed. Now we're ready to look at our species' tribal programming: the overarching behavioral framework within which we're born, live our years, and die.

Are you prepared?

Are you prepared to understand how the same creatures that can be loving, gentle, and kind, can also be brutal murderers, torturers, and rapists? And why instead of "just living in peace" we distrust, hate, and war with one another? As the Bard said, "Our fate, dear Brutus, lies not in the stars, but in ourselves." Be prepared.

We aren't, of course, used to thinking of ourselves as belonging to tribes. Yes, we know we're descendants of ancestors who belonged to tribes, and we view Africa, the Middle East, the Balkans, and some other places as still being populated by quarrelsome tribes, but as citizens of modern homogenized democracies we don't think of ourselves as belonging to a tribe ... any tribe. That's a mistake, for in fact we belong to many tribes, and we will never be able to understand ourselves until we fully understand that.

Man cannot live without tribes: we seek the sheltering security of like-behaving, like-thinking others as surely as we seek food, water, and shade. Paraphrasing John Donne, "No man is tribeless, no man survives alone." Whenever we speak of "our society" we are speaking of our primary tribe. Even when we see ourselves as loners courageously going against the tide of society, we survive only as long as society has a niche for our aberrant behavior and we don't exceed its parameters. Exceed them, cross the pale, and we are either imprisoned as insane or hunted down and killed.

"Civilization" is the process of merging tribes into ever-larger ones. When several tribes, perhaps tired of their warfare and/or threatened by a common enemy, begin to see themselves as having similar histories, interests, and goals, they may begin working together and come to think of themselves as one. As tribal size grows, villages become cities, cities become city-states, and city-states become nations. That's the benign scenario. The less benign is when better-led and more efficiently murderous tribes simply invade and incorporate lesser ones.

When civilizations break down, subtribe identities reemerge, and competition for dominance – warring – resumes: this has been convincingly demonstrated throughout human history, from the breakdown of the Greek and the Roman empires to the breakdown of colonialism and the Soviet Union. Whenever there's anarchy, whenever our primary tribe disintegrates, we seek shelter in whatever underlying tribes survive – or form new ones.

Our natural instinct to align and array ourselves tribally is omnipresent: it provides not only a framework for our existing tribes but also a template for creating new ones. Whenever our primary tribe is large enough, we evolve cultural subtribes to govern our various human activities and interests within it. The more visible ones are our political parties, religious groups, ethnic groups, city/state citizenry, school/college students and alumni, sports teams and fans, extended families, peer groups, youth gangs, etc. Each of our subtribes has its own set of tenets, but as long as the tenets don't conflict, the subtribes coexist as unconcernedly as nonthreatening species sharing the same environment. If the tenets do happen to conflict, we don't even notice and simply apply the ones most suitable to the occasion. If we're ever questioned about our inconsistencies, we become indignant, defensive, and angry ... and invent "cognitive dissonance."

When a subtribe is large enough, it too hosts subtribes. Political parties often host liberal, moderate, and conservative wings; high schools across the land host jocks, preppies, nerds, rednecks, and whatever ethnic groups feel excluded elsewhere. Whenever we don't feel accepted by the more dominant subtribes, we just keep looking until we find one that accepts us. If all else fails, we imagine ourselves part of some superior, enlightened tribe floating intellectually above the rest and deriding their lack of understanding. With the advent of the Internet, this last resort may no longer be necessary, since it's now possible to find a multitude of online subtribes to identify with – sans the trouble of conjuring one up.

By puberty most of us unconsciously identify with a whole menagerie of subtribes. Normally our first tribal identity is with our birth family, but as we mature our primary loyalty shifts from the family to other subtribes in the society. Parents of teenagers discover this with considerable dismay if the prevailing societal values clash with their family values. The shifting isn't always obvious since most families do have the same values as their society, and most societies place considerable value on children being obedient to their families and learning social values from them. If an individual in such a society betrays his family, not only his family screams in outrage but all the families in the society. If a family espouses values different from the prevailing social values, however, only family members chastise an offender, and the rest of society ignores the affront – at best – or ridicules and/or punishes the family for imposing nonconforming values on its offspring.

By adulthood our selection of tribes, chosen by natural inclination (genes) and what's available (environment), will have been augmented, sifted, sorted, and ordered into some unconscious hierarchy. All our lives are lived largely in response to the tenets, teachings, and examples of our tribes. They subconsciously control our thinking, beliefs, and acceptance of new ideas and, consequently, affect all our behavior that is learned rather than innate. It's difficult to impossible for us to maintain ideas or beliefs that aren't sanctioned by our tribe(s). If we do retain a nonconforming belief – because of a nagging conviction it's true – we deliberately suppress it to avoid the wrath of our tribe.

What, then, are the details of this hypothesized all-encompassing tribal programming that keeps us in its thrall? How does it work? I submit that the following are ten traits of human tribes – characteristics that have remained unchanged from primitive to present:

1) A common formative bond experienced over a period of time.
2) A name by which tribal members identify themselves.
3) A set of tribal tenets, including a "noble cause" and a "scapegoat enemy."
4) Instinctive fear of tampering with tribal tenets.
5) Love and sacrifice for tribal members, but no empathy or sympathy for outsiders.
6) Blind support for tribal members over outsiders.
7) Zealous defense of tribal territory and tribal tenets.

8) Member recognition based on appearance,
   behavior, and allegiance to tribal tenets.
9) Use of a rival tribe's real or imagined flaws to
   justify savaging them.
10) An instinct to dominate other tribes and impose
    beliefs on them.

Claiming there are "ten" tribal traits is arbitrary, of course. Upon reflection, you or I might think of others, or the ten could be subdivided differently to arrive at a different number. Nonetheless, let's examine these ten further.

1) A common formative bond experienced over a period of time

The formative bond may be based on common ancestry, territory, beliefs, experiences, any combination thereof, or other commonalities that "create" a tribe. It may be as dramatic as a war for independence or as innocuous as having children on the same soccer team. Practically any experience requiring a group of people to work together for a common interest over a period of time is capable of initiating tribal bonding: the greater the emotional involvement, the greater the obstacles or dangers they face, and the longer they work together – the stronger will be their bonding and the greater the likelihood that other tribal traits will manifest themselves.

2) A name by which tribal members identify themselves

Humans name things both compulsively and out of necessity. Anything without a name can't be discussed or even consciously thought about; effectively, it doesn't exist. Those sharing a formative bond come to think of themselves by a particular name or names. It comes naturally. Whenever we form a group, club, or team, the first thing we do is think up a name for it. Even in the little cliques we unconsciously form, we come to think of ourselves by some name – the Misfits, the Braintrust, the Break Bunch, the Cube Rats, etc. ... A name applied by outsiders doesn't qualify unless the tribe adopts it: "Yankee Doodle" was originally applied derisively, but American colonists liked it, adopted it, and it's now part of American history.

3) A set of tribal tenets, including a "noble cause" and a "scapegoat enemy"

Human tribes evolve a set of tenets – shared beliefs – that define the tribe and thereafter control its behavior and thinking. These beliefs take on a "sacred" or "religious" significance even when they aren't explicitly religious.

The most important of a tribe's tenets are those that describe the tribe's "noble cause" – some worthwhile goal it is striving for that justifies its continuing existence. Having a cause that is noble justifies not only a tribe's existence but also its right to dominate. We may consciously deny it, but we believe our primary tribe's noble cause justifies any and all means to achieve it ... and we behave that way.

Whatever tribe or force opposes our noble cause becomes a "scapegoat enemy" and is thereafter blamed for all setbacks to the cause. The scapegoat enemy is the embodiment of Evil. Fear of it is conjured up whenever convenient or necessary to arouse the tribe to action. Adolf Hitler wrote in *Mein Kampf*, "The art of leadership ... consists in consolidating the attention of the people against a single adversary and taking care that nothing will split up that attention. ... The leader of genius must have the ability to make different opponents appear as if they belonged to one category." Machiavelli couldn't have described a "scapegoat enemy" better.

4) *Instinctive fear of tampering with tribal tenets*

It's impossible to exaggerate the influence of tribal tenets on human behavior: they are to human tribes what the Queen Bee and Queen Ant are to insects – so essential to our existence that we instinctively swarm to defend them. They're the "glue" that holds a tribe together, and if they go, so does the tribe. The Roman historian who attributed the fall of Rome to a waning belief in traditional Roman gods was right. Our beliefs, our tribal tenets, are the armor protecting us from the onslaughts of our enemies. Question those beliefs, and we weaken our defenses, providing chinks for the enemy to pour through. Special contempt is reserved for heretics, apostates, and prophets – for anyone who questions a tribe's beliefs, even with the intent of improving them. They are far worse than the merely unenlightened enemy, for they once had the Truth and are now rejecting it!

5) *Love and sacrifice for tribal members, but no empathy or sympathy for outsiders*

Historically we have viewed only members of our own tribe as "human" and have viewed all others as something less: early tribes usually identified themselves as "the People," and other tribes as "non-People." As non-People, outsiders could be treated cruelly without qualm, conscience, or even awareness. As William Blake wrote in "A Poison Tree":

> *I was angry with my friend:*
> *I told my wrath, my wrath did end.*
> *I was angry with my foe:*
> *I told it not, my wrath did grow.*

This dichotomy in the way we treat tribe members (friends) and outsiders (foes) is the source of endless debates over whether Man is "basically good" or "basically evil." Those observing the love and sacrifice for one another within a tribe conclude we are by nature good and that evil is an aberration, while those observing our historical compulsion to war with one another conclude we are by nature evil and that good is achievable only through effort.

The truth is that by nature we are both good and evil – good to those who are like us, and evil to those who aren't: our instinct is to love our friends and to harm our foes. It has been demonstrated repeatedly – sickeningly – that whenever we cease to view others as fellow humans, as belonging to any of our tribes, we can kill them as unconcernedly as we clear land of trees and boulders. Neither Hitler's henchmen nor Jim Crow lynchers felt the slightest qualm about the murders they committed ... nor might you, given proper circumstances and improper programming.

6) Blind support for tribal members over outsiders

Our fellow tribespeople support the tribal noble cause and outsiders do not; consequently, it is right, proper, and imperative to support tribe members no matter what they do to outsiders, even if it means violating all the principles of honesty, fairness, and justice we otherwise profess. "My country, right or wrong" blatantly acknowledges this impulse. Samuel Johnson's observation that "Patriotism is the last refuge of a scoundrel" and Ambrose Bierce's emendation that it is "the first refuge" are actually subsets of the larger truth that "The only refuge for a defenseless scoundrel is the claim he acted for his tribe." An appeal to "Patriotism" serves both as an appeal to the national tribe for pardon and as an excuse for the scoundrel's political tribe to exonerate him.

This predilection to support tribe members, right or wrong, is evident from earliest childhood. To not "squeal" on our friends against outsiders comes naturally: we begin with not telling parents or teachers what's going on in our peer jungle, even when we fearfully know that telling is the only way to prevent irrevocable harm to tribemates. We don't have to be taught this – even though it becomes one of the first tenets our fledgling tribe expresses – because we instinctively feel uncomfortable telling on tribemates even for their own good. If we overcome that instinct and do tell, it only happens once because – rather than being praised by our peers for saving someone from grief – we are chastised cruelly for betraying the tribe ("Snitch!"... "Teacher's Pet!"... "Momma's Boy!"... "Tattletale!"). This instinct-cum-tenet lives on in the codes of silence proclaimed by street gangs, criminals, Mafioso and, perversely, police and fire departments. Stoically accepting punishment rather than "ratting" on guilty tribemates is considered noble, even when the result is injustice and harm to the greater society. Even vaunted professional societies supposedly policing their members' behavior more often function as protectors, keeping any malfeasance from public view and minimizing punishment of the malefactors.

This tendency – no, compulsion – to protect tribemates even when they've done wrong shows up repeatedly in our judicial and political processes. In the courts, cases of defendants being freed while obviously guilty of murdering or maiming someone of another race (tribe) are not rare, neither historically nor currently. The only "progress" that's been made in recent decades is that past injustices were always against Negro victims, and now it's as likely to be against Caucasian victims. That *equal injustice for all* is "progress" seems a telling commentary on the power of our compulsion to place tribal allegiance above justice.

The saddening truth is that no race or tribe is better than another in this respect. While a tribe is being systematically persecuted, members rightly appeal for freedom and justice, and appear to be morally superior to their oppressors – indeed, they actually are. Once free from domination, however, their desire for "freedom and justice for all" fades and is overcome by the tribal instinct to place the protection of tribal members above justice.

All tribes have their share of "racists" – members who take the tribal trait of scapegoating to the extreme – and when racists are tried for blatant crimes against outsiders, their tribe members perversely join together to subvert justice and free them. Were these crimes against people who'd actually harmed the tribe, this would be understandable; but, no, inevitably their crimes are against innocents who are as likely to be for them as against them. While it's tempting to excuse racism within minorities who have long been the victims of racism themselves – *extremely* tempting if you're a member of that minority – historically it's proven to be suicidal; as witness, the Croats and Serbs, the Israelis and Palestinians, the Protestant and Catholic Northern Irish, etc., ad nauseam.

In politics, the willingness to put the welfare of the nation (a host tribe) above one's political party (a subtribe) is called "Statesmanship" and is much praised because it is so rare – especially when the subject is whether the actions of a political leader merit punishment. When a tribal leader is involved, "Blind support for tribal members over outsiders" is magnified manyfold, since wounding a tribal leader wounds the tribe's chances for survival and dominance. Watching political tribe members engage in apoplectic contortions, distortions, and outright lies to absolve their leaders from guilt is one of democracy's more entertaining spectacles ... if you have a strong stomach.

Regrettably, but undeniably, we're all guilty of hypocrisy and double standards – they're part of our nature, manifestations of our innate bias to support tribe members against outsiders. This bias is seldom deliberate or conscious. Few of us start out with a deliberate intent to judge our race or political party's members with a lenient, forgiving set of standards and others with a harsher unforgiving set, but we end up doing it – all the while angrily denying the obvious. To accuse anyone of hypocrisy is, itself, hypocrisy.

7) *Zealous defense of tribal territory and tribal tenets*

That Man is a territorial animal fiercely defensive of his domain is well known. Before noon on Sunday December 7, 1941, the American pacifist movement had a significant and vocal following; on the morning of Monday, December 8, most of them were lined up at enlistment centers. They themselves were amazed at their visceral reaction to an attack on the American naval base at Pearl Harbor: rhetoric went out the window, and they went off to war. History tragically repeated itself on September 11, 2001, and a new generation of Americans learned firsthand the force and ferocity of emotions following an attack on one's homeland.

What's not well known is that some quirk in the way Man is wired causes us to treat our beliefs, our tribal tenets, as "territory" and to defend them with this same blind ferocity. It appears that when our augmented abilities to use language and store memories and beliefs evolved, our preexisting territorial defense programming was somehow extended to cover beliefs. This, of course, is an "as-if": we defend our beliefs with ferocity *as if* they were our territory, but it's an everyday, demonstrable reality.

The previous chapter, *Biased Man*, described how we are cued with emotional signals to automatically reject ideas threatening our beliefs or well-being: both are threatened when tribal tenets are challenged, and the emotional cue is anger. Thus when it comes to debating our tenets versus another tribe's tenets, the exercise generally degenerates into covering our ears and shouting; reason is little involved, only the desire to vanquish the enemy by means fair or foul.

Biased Man also described how our wired-in bias drives us toward polarization when our beliefs are opposed. To stretch the "territorial defense" analogy a bit, it's rather like when a citadel is expecting an attack and its defenders build walls as far out as possible to meet the enemy there rather than allowing them to approach the citadel itself. Similarly we migrate our tenets "far out" – to extremes – when they're under attack, to better defend the core.

Regardless of how we think about it or describe it, whenever our core beliefs – our tribal tenets – are challenged, we inevitably react with outrage. While our political and religious tribes demonstrate this phenomenon the most visibly, all other human institutions exhibit it as well: constant struggles between majorities defending accepted theories and minorities challenging them is the norm. Even the scientific fields, which pride themselves on objectivity and use of the Scientific Method, have a history of fiercely discounting new evidence that would usurp their territory, the prevailing theory.

8) Member recognition based on appearance, behavior, and allegiance to tribal tenets

Man, like most animals, birds, and fish, relies heavily upon appearance to initially distinguish friend from foe. Having no natural markings other than varying skin pigmentation and hair texture, we employ language, clothes, hairstyles, tattoos, body painting, and body ornaments to proclaim our tribal alliances.

Contrary to the song in the 1949 musical *South Pacific*, you don't "have to be carefully taught" to experience discomfort or fear in the presence of a stranger who looks, dresses, or acts different from you. Closeness to a stranger with different tribal markings of any sort instinctively "gets our hackles up" and "causes our skin to crawl" whether we like it or not. That reaction is instinctive, wired into us, and has nothing to do with racial prejudice. Since it undoubtedly contributed to your ancestors surviving long enough to produce you, I strongly recommend you don't attempt to override it through a misguided notion that it's unbecoming.

That initial, instinctive reaction of discomfort or fear in the presence of unrecognized persons lasts only until it's determined whether or not they're a threat: if not, subsequent encounters no longer evoke the instinctive fear; if so, subsequent encounters evoke a different fear – a justified fear of a known enemy. Racial prejudice, in contrast, is an unjustified, ongoing hatred or fear of another group: it would be better described as *Tribal* prejudice because it's really a manifestation of tribalistic "scapegoating" at its virulent worst.

Although appearance and behavior are both factors in recognizing tribal members – and affect the degree of acceptance – whether we recognize someone as "Us" or "Not Us" ultimately depends upon whether they demonstrate allegiance to our tribal tenets. Someone's appearance may be bizarre, their behavior outlandish, but if they're nonthreatening and don't violate tribal laws, we'll tolerate them as long as they believe in and support the same tenets we do; if they do, they're "Us."

Conversely, if someone appears like us, behaves like us, but espouses beliefs contrary to our tribe's tenets, we express shocked outrage at this "wolf in sheep's clothing" and angrily reject and shun him – if unable to harm him as we'd like to do. Whereas brown-rat clans identify and kill trespassing brown rats based on odor, we do so based on tenets. Question tribal tenets, whether as a prophet or a heretic, and you are anathema – and history.

9) Use of a rival tribe's real or imagined flaws to justify savaging them

To savagely destroy an enemy tribe as we would like, we need an excuse, a justification, since we don't want to see ourselves as the malevolent, murderous creatures we are. Thus we need to find some fatal "flaw" in our enemy, something serious enough to justify their subjugation (at least) or their extermination (at best). Fortunately this is fairly easy since their tribe, like ours, harbors a fair number of crazies, incendiaries, and extremists. All we need to do is wait till one of them says something outrageous about us or does something heinous toward us and – voila! – we've got them! Forever after we can describe the horror as being perpetrated not by extremist members of their tribe but by the whole tribe, a clear justification for eviscerating them mercilessly at every opportunity. And – a blessing! – there's even a tinge of truth to our subterfuge: since the other tribe won't immediately repudiate the offenders – and probably will initially defend them – our pretense that the whole tribe is like them becomes justified in our minds – Destroy!

While full-blown savagery is generally practiced only by our topmost tribes – national, political, and religious tribes – the instinct and potential lurk within subtribes too. All human groups with a distinguishing identity and some common cause, however innocent, have the potential for exhibiting more virulent tribal traits when their interests are threatened or challenged: the traits are nascent, needing only the opportunity to grow to reveal themselves. When a virulent tribal trait kicks in full force in a subtribe, it's embarrassing, and we shake our heads in bewilderment saying, "Now whatever made them behave like that?" Political and religious groups, "Sure." Neighborhood gangs and social outcasts, "Well, why not?" But sports fans? Cliques in companies and academia? Advocacy groups? Little League, soccer league, and PTA moms and dads? – shocking and inexplicable, unless you understand that tribal instincts can take over our behavior any time we don't restrain them. All it takes is a common goal being thwarted or a common belief being challenged and a leader willing to inflame followers.

10) *An instinct to dominate other tribes and impose beliefs on them*

Tribal territorial animals by definition have an instinct to vie with other tribes of their species for the best territory, but only humans have the additional burden of defending tribal beliefs as well as tribal lands, and only humans have the burden of attempting to explain these compulsions "rationally."

It could be "reasoned" that since we automatically experience fear and distrust in the presence of strangers who look, dress, or act different from us, it's only natural that we would fear and distrust whole tribes made up of such strangers. Does our desire to dominate other tribes arise solely from this fear and distrust of them, or do we harbor an independent aggressive instinct that urges us to attack others and impose our beliefs?

Nobody knows.

But we can guess, based on experiential evidence.

Our Great Explainer might argue that the only alternative to trying to dominate tribes we fear and distrust is to flee from them – abandoning our territory –

and since we're programmed to *not* do that, our only recourse is to attack them in self-defense. But then, our Great Explainer is known to be blindly committed to justifying our behavior. If our warring with other tribes *were* based only on fear and distrust of them rather than on an instinct to dominate them, it would follow that once a tribe became large enough, victorious enough, and powerful enough to no longer fear other tribes, it would no longer attack and subjugate them. The history of Man, however, documents that this is not the case.

The history of Man is a history of empires: the Assyrians, Babylonians, Greeks, Romans, Germanics, Islamics, Mongolians, Chinese dynasties, Aztecs, Mayans, European colonial empires, the United States, and most recently the Soviet Union. None of these but the United States ceased their conquering when there was no longer any need to fear attack by others, and the United States did so only after achieving its jingoist "Manifest Destiny" of stretching from the Atlantic to the Pacific. Thus, there is good reason to conclude we do indeed have an independent instinct to dominate other tribes, and that, as discussed for other traits, we do so by imposing our beliefs.

● ● ●

Imaginatively, these ten tribal traits taken together comprise a "template" for tribal behavior, and each tribe we join fills in a copy with its particular causes, scapegoats, dress codes, etc. Your first tribal identity was probably with your birth family: thirty thousand or so dice/genes were rolled, and nine months later you came tumbling into the world, naked, with nothing but your baby face and baby smile to entice them to not sacrifice you to Molach – or toss you in a dumpster. By incredible coincidence your parents were programmed to respond to your baby face and baby smile, so those of you reading this survived your first challenge.

Your family tribe had a common formative bond, the family history; a name by which they identified themselves, the family name; and a set of tenets they believed in, defended, and passed on to you – with varying degrees of success. Some family tribes even had a scapegoat enemy – a rival branch of the family or some other family, like the Hatfields & McCoys.

Your family tribe soon had competition for your loyalty. They were part of a community tribe, which was part of some locality tribe, and so on, up to a national tribe. As you grew up, you became exposed more and more to the beliefs of these other tribes and had to wrestle with which beliefs seemed right and which tribes you would eventually "join" by accepting their beliefs.

You probably had no choice in which high school you attended, so the school history, school name, and school tenets were dumped on you, just as the family tenets were. High school tenets always include a scapegoat enemy – a rival high school – and have the noble goal of beating them at everything from academics to sports. The common bond, of course, is being classmates.

But then you began to notice something new. Within your school there were bunches of neat little tribes you could choose to join or not. Besides the ethnic tribes, there were jocks, preppies, nerds/geeks, rednecks, and outsiders. To join them, all you had to do was dress and act like them, hang out with them, and adopt their beliefs – their attitudes. Since these tribes, like most, weren't particularly friendly with one another, you may even have been forced to join one just for protection from the others.

If the dress, behavior, and tenets of the tribes you chose conflicted with those of your family tribe, you and they undoubtedly exchanged many angry words and wept many hot tears. You were compelled to behave like your new primary tribe, even if it meant alienation from your family tribe.

If you went on to college, it was much like high school, except there were even more optional tribes to choose from. By selecting a major and earning a degree, you automatically joined a whole slew of academic and professional tribes, each requiring allegiance to its core teachings and expecting reasonable compliance with its standards of dress and behavior.

Once employed – during, after, or instead of college – in order to become part of the workplace tribe, you were expected to not only do your job but to buy into the company's mission statement and dress code, and to work to defeat the hated competition. And, by the way, if you could happen to make your political and religious beliefs conform to company management's, it wouldn't hurt your career any.

Regarding political and religious beliefs, throughout all of this, you were also selecting your political and religious tribes. At first you bought into your family tribe's beliefs, but as you became older and more independent you gradually – or abruptly – transferred allegiance to political/apolitical and religious/nonreligious tribes of your own choosing – to your parents' dismay if your choices differed from theirs. Since political, religious, and national tribes exhibit tribal traits more strongly than others, you are most likely to experience anger and outrage whenever these tenets are attacked.

Thus we maintain within us a hierarchical collection of tribal specifications that, as mentioned before, coexist with one another as nonchalantly as nonthreatening species sharing an environment. The tribal specification that's operative depends upon the tribe we're with and its relative importance in the hierarchy. That is, we speak, behave, and even think differently depending upon the group we're with – our family tribe, work tribe, social tribe, political tribe, religious (or irreligious) tribe, or our sports tribe. Within each we obey the appropriate dress and behavior codes, laud the noble cause, condemn the scapegoat enemy and its despicable leaders, share outrage at attacks upon our tribal tenets and leaders, and love and support one another. As we slip effortlessly, unconsciously, from one tribal setting to the next, we don't notice or care if our thinking and behavior in one setting contradicts our thinking and behavior in another. Thus we can happily enjoy risqué jokes in one setting, scorn them in another, and be blithely unconcerned with our hypocrisy.

But what happens if someone points out the contradiction between the way we behave in one setting and the way we behave in another? Well, if it's someone in our tribe, we laugh about it – automatically. Because that's the way we're wired to resolve embarrassment about inconsistencies. This is what enables humorists and comics to make a living: they point out our foibles and inconsistencies, and we laugh about them. When we're being honest within our tribes, we admit we love jokes about *other* ethnic groups, *other* religions, and the *other* political parties, but that we get upset and angry if the jokes are about *our* ethnic group, *our* religion, or *our* political party. So we laugh and enjoy our little foibles.

But if someone *not* in our tribe points out the same inconsistencies, then instead of automatically laughing, we automatically get angry, enraged, and attack both them and their arguments. Which is why comics outside our tribe don't seem the least bit funny to us.

• • •

Having now been exposed to the ten tribal traits, you will likely begin to notice almost everywhere how this tribal "programming" continuously influences your behavior: you will notice more and more how you unthinkingly, instinctively forgive friends and condemn foes for the same actions; how you envision your causes as noble and despise as evil those who question them; how you defend your beliefs fiercely and refuse to reexamine them even slightly; how you instinctively shrink from those appearing different from you and your friends, but accept them if they spout basically the same slogans you do; how you defend perpetrators of lies, slander, and malice who are "on your side" against their victims "on the other side" at the expense of proclaimed commitments to fairness and justice for all; how you point at excesses by extremists "on the other side" as representative of the other side and scream for its dismemberment, while at the same time you ignore or downplay the excesses of your own extremists – all this with wide-eyed innocence and the clearest of conscience.

Perhaps you'll also begin to notice the hierarchy of overlaid tribal tenets you maintain within you and how easily (and unconsciously) you invoke one or another depending upon which tribe you're with and how important it is to you. You may even notice that your various sets of tenets aren't always reconcilable. And that it doesn't bother you a bit.

Or you may not notice a damn thing.

You may prefer to think this is all nonsense, so you can continue perpetrating outrageous offenses against the innocent with a clear conscience.

But I hope not.

You see, the future of the human race – the *damned* human race – depends upon *your* willingness to change.

● ● ●

While this overarching tribal programming establishes the framework within which we labor – and condemns us to our endless warring – much other programming operates *within* the framework to create and govern particular characteristics of our behavior. The next eight chapters each describe one of these characteristics and the programming that governs it.

Chapter 5
Idea Man: Do Men Possess Ideas, or Do Ideas Possess Men?

"A person with a new idea is a crank until the idea succeeds." – Mark Twain

Is it not for our ideas that we live and die? Once we believe an idea to be true, do we not cease possessing it, and it instead possesses us? Evidence that we willingly die to defend and promulgate our ideas is so abundant that Richard Dawkins in his 1976 book *The Selfish Gene* introduced the provocative possibility that human brains – and consequently humans – were mere carriers for ideas that replicated, mutated, and spread in accordance with Darwinian natural selection. He dubbed this unit of cultural information a "meme," as a parallel to the DNA "gene" that replicates and occasionally mutates to drive evolution. Dawkins' idea (meme?) was picked up and furthered (replicated with mutations?) by Susan Blackmore, most notably in her 1999 book *The Meme Machine*. Naturally, our self-centered Great Explainer rejects such a humbling idea, but our observed human behavior clearly justifies the hypothesis that we are possessed by our ideas. ... Are we?

Well, yes and no.

To "possess" us, an idea must not only be considered true intellectually but must also be somehow promoted to the pantheon of beliefs – tribal tenets – that effectively *do* control our behavior. While some of that pantheon is hardwired – we don't have to be taught to be territorial and to die defending our homeland, for example, or to be prudish and feel uncomfortable talking about sex in mixed company – much of the rest is firmwired: we do have to be exposed to and choose to accept the particular political, religious, and societal beliefs we contend over. The long list of polarizing issues in Chapter 3, *Biased Man*, is actually a list of ideas that have been promoted to beliefs – tribal tenets – and consequently are fought over as blindly and fiercely as territory. That we treat ideas that have become beliefs passionately and irrationally is clear, but how the brain *accomplishes* this phenomenon – how softwired ideas become promoted to firmwired, controlling beliefs – is still unknown.

Among the things that *are* known, however, is that we are born with a hardwired predisposition to acquire a language, and that the languages we're exposed to early in life become firmwired. Knowing that, it's not unreasonable to hypothesize we may also be born with a predisposition to acquire beliefs – political, religious, and societal – and that the ones we're exposed to and accept become firmwired. Making an "as-if" out of this: It's *as if* we're born with hardwired slots that must get filled in with political, religious, and societal ideas. Our predisposition (genes) and environment would then determine, consciously or unconsciously, the particular ideas we accept as beliefs and subsequently allow to control us. It's often been noted, for example, that avowedly atheistic states nonetheless have dogmas and rituals that exactly mirror religious ones. The religious "slots" have to be filled in with something; they won't go away.

All this hypothesis does, of course, is shift from the notion of ideas *somehow* being promoted to beliefs to the notion of preexisting belief slots *somehow* being filled in with selected ideas. That annoying "*somehow*" won't soon go away, for we're a long way from deciphering the brain's secrets to that degree. But I hope you're beginning to notice that the *somehows* required for a programming theory of human behavior are an improvement over the *somehows* required for complexes, ids, egos, et al. The significant thing, however, isn't *how* the brain promotes ideas to beliefs but the fact that it *does*: we don't become possessed by (we don't kill and die for) mere ideas – only beliefs.

• • •

That hardly means that "mere" ideas aren't important; they're the means through which we create our literature, art, and architecture, our music, math, and medicines, our sciences, philosophies, and religions – everything that raises us above other primates. So let's look now at the brain function that enables the manipulation of ideas: language.

The possession of language gives humans a remarkable advantage over other animals: it enables us to *think* – to process ideas consciously, critically, and analytically. Despite past claims that Man's opposing thumbs and/or erect walking were key to giving us an evolutionary advantage, it is probable that language is the significant difference between other primates and us. Although it's sometimes argued that other primates *do* possess a language capability akin to ours – because they can be trained to recognize symbols or sign-language gestures and manipulate them into meaningful phrases –

they never develop that skill in the wild, never advance beyond the level of a two- to three-year-old human, and never teach the learned skills to their offspring. Thus it appears likely that the difference in language capability between humans and other primates is more than "just a matter of degree" but involves a significant evolutionary change. While all primates may have the necessary precursors of language, only in humans has some additional evolutionary adaptation occurred to allow the flowering of a full-blown rich and complex language ability.

Unfortunately, the phrase "experts disagree" pretty well sums up opinion on how and when humans evolved their superior language capabilities, what features of the brain's language areas are responsible for them, and why other primates haven't developed greater language skills. So far there isn't any "smoking gun" that everyone can point to and exclaim, "Aha! That's why human language – and consequently thinking – is so advanced!"

It was once thought that the size of language-related brain structures might be responsible, but most researchers now agree there aren't really any significant structural differences. Instead, they're examining the microcircuits comprising the structures, looking for differences in the way we're wired. Early findings claim that the microcircuits in the language structures of human brains are different both in composition and in lateralization (the degree to which the left hemisphere's microcircuits are larger than the right's). Whether or not these wiring differences will turn out to be the sought-after explanatory difference remains to be seen.

Regardless, our possession of language enables our advanced conscious thinking – the processing of ideas. While we can consciously think to a limited degree by imagining actions – as a chimpanzee can envision placing a box beneath a dangling banana in order to reach it – to achieve creative, critical, analytical reasoning requires the ability to express not only single ideas but endless interactions of ideas – kaleidoscopes of ideas within ideas linking to still more ideas. Language conveys that ability.

And also limits it.

If our language doesn't contain words to accurately describe something we experience, then we can't describe it. That's why we fall back on, "Well, the Greeks have a word for it" – or the French or the Germans – and why translators sometimes have difficulty translating concepts from one language to another. The fact that Greek has words for various kinds of love, from erotic to selfless, and English has but one, has spawned many a footnote in the Greek-to-English translations of the Bible.

It's also why professions, industries, crafts, and regions have vernaculars to provide the terminology, nuances, and buzz words necessary to express their concepts adequately. We simply can't think about things our language has no words to describe: in order to do so we have to extend the language. Every scientific and academic field has its own specialized language to enable thinking about and expressing its precepts with greater precision. It's been said that the Inuit (Eskimos) have many words describing various types and gradations of ice and snow since their lives have historically depended upon describing such conditions accurately.

We cannot think without words. The words "We," "cannot," "think," and all other words, even the lowly conjunctions, are self-contained ideas: each conjures up a concept of some entity, action, modification, or relationship. Dictionaries are nothing more than descriptions of the ideas represented by words. And language provides us the magical ability to string ideas together effortlessly, yet in accordance with often complex rules, to create higher, more complex ideas and then to encapsulate those new ideas with a single word. *Duty. Honor. Patriotism. Love. Mercy. Sacrifice. Peace. Hope. Goodness. Liberty.*

Utterly amazing.

Ideas, you see, do not merely express thoughts; they are the basic units of thought, the *means* by which we think. Ideas are by definition conscious; if they aren't conscious, if they can't be articulated, they're not ideas, they're feelings.

Initially Man's ideas encapsulated survival and "how-to" strategies in the form of proverbs, folk sayings, wisdom teachings, tribal lore. This, most critically, allowed tribes to pass on their lore so that knowledge and understanding could accrue from generation to generation. Over the millennia Man added writing to his repertoire, and the pace of knowledge accumulation grew. The invention of the printing press accelerated it further, allowing ideas to be quickly and widely disseminated. Then came radio, television, the Internet, and, increasingly, pocket devices/computers incorporating combinations of Internet access, satellite phones, and video cameras. Each in turn has enabled the spreading of ideas more widely, more quickly than ever before in human history.

Too bad this isn't purely a good thing.

The rub is that not all ideas being spread so quickly are good: some are false; others are hateful, harmful, and destructive. Technology is stunningly amoral; it knows nothing of good and evil. All it does is amplify our tendencies toward both. The Internet illustrates this perfectly, serving as a conduit for learning, knowledge, wisdom ... and filth: it's like a combination water main and sewer pipe, both feeding and poisoning. Like all other technological advances, advances in communication do nothing to change us: we're still the same eons-old animal – just better equipped to do harm.

"So what good do our conscious, lofty softwired ideas do," you might worriedly ask, "if our hardwired natures and firmwired beliefs still unconsciously drive us toward self-destruction? Can't we ever achieve world peace?"

"That's a very good question," I might reply, attempting to sound wise. "Let's examine it further."

• • •

Can our hardwired or firmwired programming be modified sufficiently to achieve world peace? Our hardwired (tribal species) programming probably cannot. Although it's fun to fantasize about futuristic genetic engineering quelling our more nasty traits, the prospect of that occurring does not augur well for three reasons.

First, everything about us has always proved vastly more complex than first imagined. It's very likely we'll find that our tribal behavior is not governed by a single or a few genes but by complex interactions of many genes, and that manipulating them will produce unexpected and, well, undesired results.

Second, can you imagine growing up and at some point discovering you're not a beloved child but a closely monitored experiment expected to exhibit superior qualities, or else ... what? It would likely be discovered that before the experiments could continue, the tendency to commit suicide under hopelessly inhuman conditions would have to be engineered out.

And third, isn't it a bit obvious that some semblance of world peace is a *prerequisite* for attempting behavior-modifying genetic engineering? Otherwise "good" tribes would be producing pacifists and "bad" tribes would be producing superior warriors bent on killing them. Breeding pacifists may be a good thing, but without world peace it's not too bright.

That leaves us with only our firmwired programming as a possible means of overcoming our natures and allowing our lofty softwired ideas and ideals to flourish free from war. Is there any hope here?

The answer is "Yes, but only the barest."

The answer is "Yes" because, in retrospect, it can be realized that firmwired beliefs – in the guise of Wisdom and Reason – have *always* been providing a means of overriding our destructive hardwired tendencies; the answer is "but only the barest" because despite millenniums of trying, firmwired beliefs have never yet overcome our hardwired tendency to war.

It's not coincidental that for millennia Wisdom and Reason have been personified as feminine voices, calming, soothing, counseling, and redirecting angry, aggressive, self-destructive male impulses. When promoted to firmwired beliefs, wisdom teachings have been the "civilizing" influences that have raised us above the brutish, barbaric lawlessness that history has recorded we're capable of – a triumph of firmwired programming over hardwired, but woefully inadequate. It's been reasonably successful within tribes but has failed where it's needed most – between tribes. The Wisdom and Reason of one tribe has no meaning to other tribes with differing histories and cultures. In fact, since firmwired beliefs become part of a tribe's tenets, they are part of what separates them, what they want to impose upon one another. Even though their wisdom teachings may be largely identical – human nature being the same everywhere – the differing historical and cultural settings in which they're imbedded make them appear different.

Complicating the problem even more is the previously explained difficulty of altering firmwired programming: once firmwired programming – including our beliefs – is established, it requires traumatic circumstances and/or great effort to change. The "easiest" means of ensuring particular programming is by limiting the selection of ideas available for promotion to beliefs during the formative years. This, of course, is the method used by police states and tyrannical dictators but is shunned by democracies. Having observed the evils wrought when "bad" programming is imposed on societies, democracies hesitate to impose even "good" programming – particularly since we can't agree on what that programming might be.

So, yes, there *is* hope of eventually being able to bend our firmwired programming to the task of overcoming our hardwired tendency to war. But the hope is slim since it appears this is possible only if we – *all* of us, all nations and societies – come to see ourselves as having a *compelling* interest in becoming "one tribe." That is slim hope, indeed.

• • •

Throughout this chapter we've been discussing ideas: whether we possess ideas or ideas possess us; how language enables ideas to be magically joined in myriad ways to generate ever more ideas; and how "proper" ideas promoted to beliefs might conceivably overcome Mankind's propensity to war. What we haven't discussed yet about ideas is where they come from. *How* do we generate ideas? Do we just make them up? The next chapter, *Make-Up Man*, will consider the possibility that we do just that.

Chapter 6
Make-Up Man: What We Don't Know, We Make Up – Then Believe

"Many a small thing has been made large by the right kind of advertising." – Mark Twain

An astonishing amount of what we think is "known" is simply made up. If we don't know the explanation for something, we make one up – out of nothing – and if it sounds at all plausible, we immediately forget we made it up and believe it to be Truth. Making things up is one of Man's most prominent traits, and being unaware that we do so is one of the most startling. Fortunately, the discovery of our brain's Great Explainer function now allows us to recognize the source of this phenomenon, but we're still coming to grips with its extensiveness.

In the past, we only tacitly admitted we made things up, describing it not as an omnipresent human characteristic but as a mere error in logic: "*Post hoc ergo propter hoc*" or "After this, therefore because of this." This famous fallacy is described as "the mistake of assuming that some earlier event or circumstance is the *cause* of some later event or circumstance without adequate evidence to support that conclusion." The examples given usually cite the fallacy's role in politics – "My opponent has been mayor for four years, and in that time property taxes have doubled" – and as a source of superstitions – "When I carry my good-luck charm, I always do better in tests."

Two things are omitted from the literature, however: The first is a blunt admission that whenever we don't have an explanation for something we make one up, and a post hoc argument is both convenient and convincing. The other is an admission that post hoc reasoning is actually often reasonable and is probably an important part of our learning programming. When we see one event closely follow another, we're wired to automatically make up the explanation that the first event caused the second event. And why not? It's only a fallacy when it's *not* true, and much of the time it *is* true. And if we call our made-up explanation a "hypothesis" and add rigorous testing to assure the results are repeatable, suddenly it becomes the "Scientific Method." Some view it as sweet irony that Superstition and Science both spring from the same cauldron, our compulsion to make up explanations for the unknown.

A corollary to the notion that we're predisposed to generate post hoc reasoning should be that we're also predisposed to be swayed by it. We usually accept it uncritically, almost eagerly. Our unconscious programming must be aware of our susceptibility because we so regularly, effortlessly, and naturally use post hoc reasoning to mislead and deceive one another. While post hoc may actually be a "logical mistake" when fomenting superstitions, when used for political or other persuasion it's generally a ploy. We're incredibly good at selecting facts and figures judiciously to paint whatever cause-and-effect portrait we want.

The post hoc fallacy isn't the only mechanism in the Great Explainer's make-up kit; it's merely the most documented. Another is the "Somebody Else Did It" conviction. It's charming and endearing when we see a sweet-faced, innocent child looking up at us and explaining seriously how somebody else must have broken the flower vase, even though there was no one else in the house. We're less amused when we lose something, like our car keys, and we're absolutely certain someone else, probably our spouse or roommate, moved them because we certainly didn't, and we *always* put them in a particular place. Never mind that we're aware our nonspeaking half-brain sometimes performs motor actions while our speaking (conscious) half-brain is distracted and doesn't notice. If, for example, we're expecting an important call and the phone's ringing while we're trying to get into the house with an armful of groceries, we can lay down our keys to free a hand to open the door and have absolutely no conscious knowledge of doing it. Instead, we'll make up the explanation that *somebody* moved or took our keys, and will fervently believe it – until two days later when we spot them and shamefacedly realize what happened. The epithet "half-brained behavior" is sometimes more apropos than realized.

Another mechanism in the make-up kit is "I Know Your Motivation." People may try to fool us about why they're doing something, but we know better; the "truth" springs unbidden and fully formed into our minds. "You're only telling me this for my own good? Ha! You've always been jealous of me and now you're trying to hurt me." ... "You're really sorry you can't come to visit this month because ... Right! But you always make time to visit so-and-so. You just don't care as much about me as you do him."

And as always, politics ratchets up the fervor. No matter what a despised politician of an opposing party does, we "instinctively" see through his rhetoric and discern his nefarious underlying motives, and if he should do the opposite, well, we'll see through that too – even if he does things we laud members of our own party for doing. We'll attack him anyway because we'll *know* he's only doing it as a self-serving ploy. We are prepared to make up – and believe – base or Machiavellian reasons for anything and everything an opposing politician does and, for that matter, anybody else we don't like, or who disagrees with our beliefs. We do it effortlessly. The Great Explainer is ever facile, ever convincing ... and ever present.

Another mechanism in the make-up kit is "denial." Whenever addictions drive someone to compulsive, destructive, unplanned behavior, the Great Explainer is right there to generate explanations for why the behavior was harmless, really was planned, or was just a whim. Nothing short of an en masse "intervention" by all the family and friends who care for the helpless addict can get him to begrudgingly accept he really does have a serious problem and is out of control.

Fortunately, not all of the Great Explainer's activities are harmful: as already noted, add rigorous testing of our made-up hypotheses and the process becomes the Scientific Method. Does this mean Science is inoculated against our "Make it up and believe it" phenomenon? Unfortunately, no.

First, all "sciences" are *not* created equal: there are degrees to which they deserve the title "Science." Once, it was possible to think of the sciences as rungs on a "life ladder," with those dealing with lifeless matter (physics, inorganic chemistry) as the lowest rungs and moving on up through those dealing with increasingly complex life forms (organic chemistry, biology, zoology) to culminate in the social sciences dealing with humans and human endeavors (psychiatry, psychology, sociology, economics). It was then a truism that as we moved up the ladder it became increasingly difficult to test hypotheses and prove theories, and when we got to the social sciences it became – for all practical purposes – frequently impossible.

At that point it should have dawned on someone, or everyone, that if a field's theories could not be rigorously tested and proved, it was by definition not a Science and should relocate to the Humanities. But that didn't happen. Thus I sometimes refer to the social sciences as "pseudosciences," not to deny their legitimacy or value as disciplines, but to remind us that when a field's theories cannot be tested, it's no longer a Science. The distinguishing characteristic of a nonscientific field is its being splintered into many schools (factions) having minimal agreement, and all the social sciences exhibit this characteristic.

Being nontestable, the social sciences harbor an eclectic mix of truths, half-truths, and sincerely believed nonsense, all on an equal footing – rather like Religion. The less a hypothesis can be tested, it seems, the more vehemently it's believed. Too often the social sciences make up complex, unprovable theories about human social behavior, rely upon the credentials and charisma of their practitioners to garner acceptance, and consequently provide false hope that rationality will save us, even while irrationality devours us. White lab coats often serve the same function as black priestly robes. The social sciences provide the comforting illusion that we know more about our natures than we really do.

Social sciences are no longer the only nontestable sciences, however. As Science has become increasingly more detailed and complex, it has become increasingly less possible to do cutting-edge research with mere curiosity and off-the-shelf hardware. Scientific advances are now frequently delayed pending the development of new tools and technologies capable of exploring the new territories. Thus, on the cutting edge of science in any field, it usually takes years if not decades of patient, painstaking research before enough hard data accrues to prove one theory over another. The original rungs of Science's "life ladder" have morphed into horizontal tree trunks branching into hierarchies of subdisciplines, and some of the branches of historically testable disciplines now bear fruit – theories – that are difficult to impossible to test: cosmology, particle physics, and theoretical physics (a hybrid of physics and extreme math) are examples. Most of these exotic sciences harbor multiple competing theories that can't readily be tested, but – unlike the social pseudosciences – they are usually cognizant of this reality and acknowledge that until technological advances provide more data, they're just unproven hypotheses.

The true – that is, verifiable – sciences in between the pseudo and the exotic are also "in between" in honesty: generally they're objective and honest, but all have suffered episodes where theory was treated as fact, and dissenting data was ignored or suppressed. Some of those episodes will be discussed in Chapter 12, *Spiritual Man,* while examining the Science vs. Religion controversy. The reality is that we humans, scientists or not, can't help ourselves: we are programmed so that our existing beliefs – theories – automatically bias us against altering them, and especially so when we have a vested interest in the existing beliefs. That's why Behaviorism has had such a long, lingering death, and pockets of it still remain. Even with the Scientific Method as a polestar, our compulsion to make things up and believe them with insufficient evidence can overcome even that guiding principle.

Clearly, Man abhors a vacuum as much as Nature does. Whenever there's a gap in our knowledge, we inevitably make up something to fill it in. "We don't know" is not in our lexicon. And just as clearly, the things we make up inevitably support and justify our tribes' beliefs, goals, and interests – and blame, slander, and defame our scapegoat enemies. The Great Explainer über alles.

• • •

Since we're gifted – or cursed – with the ability to make things up unconsciously, it's hardly surprising we began to employ that same talent consciously – as storytelling. The next chapter, *Storytelling Man*, examines this unique human trait and its role in human society.

Chapter 7
Story-Telling Man: How We Transmit Cultural Values

"Wit is the sudden marriage of ideas which before their union were not perceived to have any relation."
– Mark Twain

It is recognized that for millennia storytelling was Man's primary means of passing on tribal history. No matter what your race, your ancestors sat around campfires or lodge fires and told and retold stories of their tribe's history: the stories described how the tribe came into being and told of its deities, heroes, villains, triumphs, and tragedies. Often the stories were memorized and passed on word-for-word from generation to generation. Even the advent of the printing press didn't change this much, for the stories were still told and retold at festival holidays and gatherings throughout the year.

What hasn't been recognized, or at least hasn't been much commented upon, is that these stories have also been Man's primary means of passing on *behavioral standards* to succeeding generations ... of seeding the ideas desired and destined to become firmwired beliefs. The stories provide inspirational examples of bravery, character, morals, and ethics being courageously practiced by the tribe and tribe members in spite of opposition, and the backgrounds of the stories illustrate what a normative society should or shouldn't be. Thus, the stories reflect not only what the tribe was and is, but also what it will become.

Our storytelling has been going on a rather long time: it isn't known when Man developed language and conscious thought, but it's generally accepted that it was over fifty thousand years ago. It's probable that both language and the means to store the flood of ideas that language generates evolved together, and that during that same time existing territorial programming adapted and evolved to be possessive of ideas as well as territory. Again, this isn't known, but if not probable, it's at least plausible.

Anyway, it doesn't matter.

What matters is that somehow, at sometime in the distant past, we ended up with language, conscious thought, treatment of ideas as territory, and storytelling; what matters is that for so many tens of thousands of years storytelling has been our means of passing on tribal lore and behavioral standards that it may well have become wired-in as our preferred means of learning acceptable behavior – of learning the ideas that become firmwired and curb our hardwired animal instincts.

The advent of writing didn't change this; it merely added a new way of "telling" the stories. Writing is a consciously contrived skill that developed a mere five or six thousand years ago. We have no genetic, wired-in predisposition to write, as we do to speak: we learn to speak effortlessly, but we have to be taught to write. In most modern societies, writing and reading have become the primary means of "telling" stories, one to another. In schools, for example, textbooks tell the stories, and teachers provide exposition, examples, and encouragement.

The acting out of tribal stories through dance and song probably long preceded writing, but writing enabled it to become "theater." Acting, like writing, is a way of "telling" stories, and the advent of theater, movies, and television enhanced rather than diminished the role of storytelling. Movies and television played for theater the same role the printing press played for literature: it allowed the rapid, widespread dissemination of stories to massive audiences.

That storytelling is an efficient and effective means of introducing ideas that eventually become beliefs is attested to by its heavy use in religious writings. The most meaningful teachings in all the major religions take the form of stories: Judaism, Christianity, Islamism, Buddhism, Hinduism, Confucianism, et al., all have bodies of stories that convey their teachings far better than do their doctrines. This is because stories have two major advantages over laws, rules, and doctrines: First, they get around our instinctive rejection of ideas that challenge our existing beliefs by not revealing their challenge until the climax of the story. And second, they add the ingredient that is essential for natural learning – emotion.

Although neuroscientists are still laboring to unravel and understand all of the observed interactions between the emotion-forming and memory-forming structures of the brain, it is generally accepted that emotion plays an important, perhaps enabling, role in memory and learning. Laws, rules, and doctrines are generally emotionless and dry, but when we read or hear stories of people involved in situations that require a decision or a response, we empathetically envision ourselves in those circumstances and share their emotions – and we learn, naturally, the way we're programmed to learn.

As a teaching/learning/programming tool, storytelling isn't limited to religions; it's omnipresent. Whenever we want to impart teachings intended to become internalized beliefs, we use storytelling. Even short proverbs are often mini-stories enabling us to envision ourselves in the action – "Look before you leap" – and to learn from it. Although some folk and fairy tales are intended only to entertain, most have morals and are intended to teach; the collections of stories we provide our children are good examples: *Aesop's Fables, Grimm's Fairy Tales, Mother Goose Tales,* and *Tales of Uncle Remus: The Adventures of Brer Rabbit.*

Arguably, *all* of our storytelling – all genres of literature and theater – portraying creatures experiencing *anything* and reacting to it is teaching us *something* about how to behave – rightly or wrongly, knowingly or unknowingly. The classics of literature are classics because, in addition to enthralling us with memorable writing, they teach us something important about ourselves: they illuminate our behavioral tendencies and their tragicomic consequences. "All the world's a stage, and all the men and women merely players." Yes, and our stories do more than document our past behaviors; they provide scripts for our future behavior.

The stories most influential to a society's future, of course, are those that originate within the society and define its history, ethos, and envisioned destiny. Literature from outside the society, world literature, generally does not have as much influence since to become world literature, stories must teach lessons applicable to people everywhere – not just one society – and thus do not often become part of a particular society's "script."

There are three notable exceptions to this, however: One is when the majority of a society's founders adhere to a particular world religion, and teachings from that religion consequently permeate the society's history. Another is when popular morality tales, like the aforementioned collections of folk and fairy tales, migrate and become part of the folklore of many societies. A third is when a subgroup within a society becomes possessed by a world idea and succeeds in convincing or coercing its society to adopt that world idea. An example of the latter is when antislavery thinking swept the Western world in the 1800s, was taken up by abolitionist groups in the United States, and after some "unpleasantness" became a permanent and revered part of America's script.

The stories that define a society and script its future might be described as "traditional," "contemporary," and "operative." Traditional stories originate during or shortly after significant events in a society's history – typically its founding and definitive struggles, and particularly its wars. Contemporary stories are grounded in traditional stories and values, but extrapolate them to current conditions and concerns. Operative stories are the subset of traditional and contemporary stories that reflect the society's currently *operative* beliefs; that is, what is actually believed and practiced, as opposed to what's proclaimed but not practiced. Thus it is the operative stories that form the "script" for the society's future.

Traditional stories embody and idealize the society's tribal tenets and aspirations, particularly its noble cause and scapegoat enemy; they deliberately gloss over blemishes in the society's history and heroes in order to provide better examples to emulate. That's necessary and wise, for if a society's founders and heroes are portrayed as flawed, how could their descendents be expected to be any better?

Contemporary stories, however, may either reinforce or *challenge* traditional stories and values. Whenever there is disagreement over the future direction of a society, the contending groups vie to have stories reflecting their ideals and ideologies predominate. These Herculean efforts to influence which stories are accepted as "true" reveal our intuitive knowledge that those stories – or, more accurately, the ideas they embody – will affect our future: therefore, leaders in human societies everywhere attempt to control which contemporary stories predominate. In closed societies the first act of a new dictator is to take control of all forms of media – radio, television, movies, plays, newspapers, magazines, and books – and the next act is to have them begin pouring out stories glorifying the regime.

Open societies are more interesting, particularly those having two or more major political parties competing for dominance in regular elections. Each election is a battle over whose tribal tenets will prevail and whose preferred contemporary stories will become the operative ones. Beneath the cyclical battles, however, is a more important – and generally unremarked – war for long-term dominance. If one party's tenets prevail long enough, or if traumatic events imprint them, some of that party's tenets will permeate and become part of the national tribal tenets, and thus become accepted as unquestioned "truth" by the majority of the nation, except, of course, the disgruntled core members of the opposition party. Ideas and behavior buttressing the national tribal tenets are approved and applauded, and ideas and behavior questioning or challenging them are ridiculed and ostracized. The apt phrase "politically correct" has been coined to describe this phenomenon.

What is politically correct effectively determines which laws are obeyed and disobeyed. The laws that are "on the books" do not matter as much as the ones that are enforced, and the politically correct operative stories reflect which laws are believed in strongly enough to be enforced, and upon whom they will be enforced. If operative stories and anecdotes portray officially outlawed behavior as acceptable, that behavior will be practiced regardless of laws and lip service to the contrary (see Prohibition), and if they portray officially approved behavior as unenlightened and foolish, that behavior will not be practiced unless imposed.

Changes in the *dominant* political party, as opposed to the *prevailing* political party, do not occur very quickly or very often. As long as a party retains the ability to dictate what is politically correct, it is the de facto "dominant" party, even if it loses a series of election battles. It could be argued, for example, that in the United States the Republican party was dominant from the 1860s to the 1920s, and the Democratic party from the 1930s to the present: although the Republican party, as of this writing, occupies the Whitehouse and has a majority in both houses of Congress, the Democratic party still dictates what is politically correct.

There are at least three factors that slow down reversals of dominance: one, of course, is our wired-in resistance to changing currently accepted beliefs; a second is the existence of bureaucracies having vested interests in the current regime; and a third is the tendency of academia and intelligentsia to institutionalize ideas once they have embraced them. These factors provide an inertia that prolongs acceptance and retention of a dominant political party's tenets as part of the national tenets.

While it is sometimes claimed that democracies go through political cycles every "X" number of years, democracies really have not been around long enough to establish any typical duration: it is possible that changes in dominance depend more upon circumstances and galvanizing events than cycles. One certainty, however, is that storytelling is an essential element in these struggles for dominance. Far from being merely for communication and entertainment, storytelling is our primary source of softwired programming destined to become firmwired behavioral programming, and political and religious tribes contend relentlessly to bias the content.

A concluding caveat: it has not yet been *proven* that the ideas, values, and behaviors portrayed in books, plays, movies, and television subconsciously program us – that is, teach us to accept them as normative and to subsequently alter our behavior in their direction – just as at one time it was not *proven* that germs and microbes in our offal could harm us. But they could, and did, in spite of our ignorance of what was happening.

"Consequently," I say, "whenever irrational, animalistic behavior is portrayed and glorified in the entertainment media, it is extremely likely that it will similarly poison our societies, and enlightened censorship may be a necessity."

"But," you may say smugly, "you can't prove it!"

And of course, I can't. This is in the arena of pseudoscience, where it's extremely difficult to prove anything substantial because we can't conduct large-scale tests on human societies to see how things affect them. All that's available is the "anecdotal evidence," which is necessarily subjective, and which different groups with different motivations see ... differently.

Nonetheless, you have been warned.

• • •

Underlying Man's storytelling ability is another ability – one that is prerequisite for storytelling: it is the ability to encapsulate complex concepts into symbols, to effectively tell an entire "story" with a single word or image. The next chapter, *Symbolic Man*, will examine this trait.

Chapter 8
Symbolic Man: Encapsulating Concepts

"Cauliflower is nothing but cabbage with a college education." – Mark Twain

Man has the ability to represent complex ideas – concepts – with simple symbols that deliver the same content and emotional impact as the concept itself. A mere dollar sign, "$," conjures up the concept "money," and the single word *money* conjures up the concept of currency and how it's used. Indeed, as discussed in Chapter 5, *Idea Man*, *all* the words we use are symbols that encapsulate their definitions. This chapter will demonstrate how widespread our use of symbolism is, how symbols can take on more emotional impact and power than the things they represent, and how our use of symbols has some pitfalls.

Animal brains began employing symbols as shorthand well before language developed in humans. For example, the silhouette of a bird of prey is a symbol that sends small birds and animals scampering for cover: in laboratory settings a black cardboard cutout resembling a predator's silhouette will trigger the birds' fear-and-hide response whenever it's displayed above them.

Once Nature is onto a technique that works, it doesn't hesitate to incorporate it elsewhere, so, not surprisingly, we find symbols incorporated widely in our processing of visual and audio input. To illustrate, here are five arbitrary categories of symbol usage, followed by brief discussions of the symbols in each category:

Language – Words; slogans, mottos; creeds; references
Body   – Facial expressions; postures; gestures
Dress   – Decorative items; hairstyles; uniforms
Graphic   – Flags, emblems; logos, icons; color combinations
Music   – Rhythms; phrases, themes; songs; anthems

Language Symbolism

- **Words** – As discussed in Chapter 5, all words are symbols that encapsulate their definitions.
- **Slogans, Mottos** – Phrases or sentences that encapsulate a thought or concept can become symbols in the same way words become symbols for their definitions. "Satisfaction Guaranteed" symbolizes a commitment by a proprietor or marketer to either provide a good service or product to customers or to make it up to them in some way. "Be Prepared," the oft-quoted Boy Scout motto, symbolizes always having ready the tools and attitude to handle whatever life throws at you. "Remember the Alamo ... the Maine ... Pearl Harbor ... 9/11" symbolize both a desire to avenge an attack and the perils of complacency.
- **Creeds** – Creeds encapsulate important beliefs of a tribe or group; once they're established and referenced by a name, the name becomes symbolic for the entire set of beliefs. Creeds are usually associated with religions, but secular documents like the *Preamble to the United States Constitution* and *The Bill of Rights* are essentially creeds.

· **References** - Simply referring to something already known evokes all the memories and emotions associated with it:

Stories – Many stories and books have well-known major themes, and thus stories and books can become symbols for their themes. *Uncle Tom's Cabin* is a symbol for antislavery and the evils of slavery; *War and Peace* is a symbol for both humanity's epic struggle with inhumanity ... and for very long books; *Pilgrim's Progress* is a symbol for religious growth, and for allegorical books.

People – The names of people who become famous – or infamous – in history, literature, or the evening news become symbols for the philosophy, trait, or action associated with them. Benedict Arnold forever symbolizes treason; Abe Lincoln, honesty; Thomas Edison, invention; Martin Luther King Jr., civil rights; Charles Lindbergh, brave pioneering. Some are so symbolic of their associated behavior that they become adjectival: Machiavelli and Machiavellian, Keynes and Keynesian, Nietzsche and Nietzschean.

Events – The names of historically noteworthy events, particularly ones associated with ushering in a new era, often become symbols for the accompanying human drama: Magna Carta, Independence Day, Kristallnacht, D-day.

Places – The names of the places where traumatic or historically noteworthy events occurred often become symbols for the events: Agincourt, Gettysburg, Little Big Horn, Normandy, Hiroshima, Woodstock, Malta, Bay of Pigs.

Brand Names – Marketers earn their money when they succeed in making a brand name not only the well-known name of a product, business, or service, but a symbol of quality – to use a currently well-known example, the "Cadillac" of such products, businesses, and services. Over the years various brand names have achieved such renown. With apologies to the many omitted, some that have enjoyed long renown in America are: Ivory soap, Gillette razors, Gold Medal flour, Goodyear tires, Kodak cameras and film, Budweiser beer, Hyatt hotels, etc.

Body Symbolism

- **Facial Expressions** – It has become well known that we employ species-wide/world-wide common facial expressions for fear, distress, surprise, sadness, joy, anger, disgust, and interest: these expressions become symbols for the emotions they represent. Amazingly, most of them can be recognized by babies as young as three weeks old.
- **Postures** – In any culture around the world, primitive or modern, we find we can perceive the attitudes, moods, and dispositions of people just from the familiar, symbolic way they stand, walk, sit, or repose. ... Ask any mime.
- **Gestures** – Many gestures, such as raising a hand in greeting or waving a hand in parting, are species-wide; but many others are cultural, which is why we stereotype how much or how little other nationalities use gestures, and *how* they use them.

Dress Symbolism

- **Decorative Items** – Not all of the decorative pins and jewelry we adorn ourselves with are for show; many symbolize our allegiance to some cause, movement, or tribe.

- **Hairstyles** – Hairstyles are particularly good for symbolic subtribal identification, and youth, in particular, appreciate the power of a subtribe's hairstyle to not only set them apart but to annoy those not in their subtribe. Hence, the Longhairs, Skinheads, Ponytails, etc.
- **Uniforms** – The purpose of uniforms, of course, *is* to be symbolic, and they take many forms – from formal uniforms to informal use of almost any distinctive garb. Even "Suits" and "Blue Collars" can become uniforms, as well as the garish attire of breakaway subtribes.

Graphic Symbolism

- **Flags, Emblems** – We rally 'round the flag, boys and girls, men and women, and we don't care if it's a national flag, school flag, corporate flag, or any of the other flags representing one of our tribes.
- **Logos, Icons** – It's a poor organization, indeed, that hasn't a logo, a stylized symbol to represent it, and we'd have trouble finding the proper restroom – or computer program – without an icon to cue us.
- **Color Combinations** – The color combinations from flags, logos, etc., often become as symbolic as the flags and logos themselves. Even single colors can become symbolic: IBM is known as "Big Blue," and in imperial Rome, the colors green, blue, red, and white became symbols of four chariot-racing teams and their followers.

Music Symbolism

- **Rhythms** – Beat out that rhythm on a drum ... and it will symbolize much: tom-toms, marital beats, waltz beats, Latin beats, syncopated rhythms ... all will conjure up the worlds associated with them.

- **Phrases, Themes** – Mere phrases from musical pieces or themes from plays and movies can recall to us not only the essence of the entire piece but also what it represents.
- **Songs** – Songs often express facets of our human experience: joy and happiness, trials and sorrow, finding love or losing it, adventures, peace, sagas, journeys, battles and bravery, victories and defeats, birth songs and requiems. Every song becomes a symbol for the story it tells, and some songs become symbols of the eras they celebrated.
- **Anthems** – Songs that celebrate tribes and their noble causes.

• • •

Besides their incredibly widespread use in human culture, the next most remarkable thing about symbols is their ability to evoke responses and emotions even greater than the concepts they symbolize. Two things seem to enable this: the first is that it is possible – some say probable – that everything stored in our brain's memory has an associated emotional component, positive or negative; the second is that symbols can come to represent not merely a concept but the pure, perfect, and concentrated essence of the concept. Plato was aware of this property of symbols and immortalized it with his hypothesis of preexisting, idealized "Forms" that allow us to recognize less-than-perfect earthly objects. We now can recognize that Plato had it reversed and that his "Forms" are actually the symbols that result when our brain distills out the abstract perfect essence of the objects and concepts we encounter. Such symbols often evoke stronger emotional reactions than single instances of the objects or concepts themselves. It would seem that these symbols, as the concentrated essence of all the contributing instances, also have the concentrated emotional impact of them all.

Symbols that represent "Us" – particularly national emblems – fall into this category and consequently become extremely emotional extensions of ourselves; attacking them is more than attacking us; it's attacking our very essence. It is no wonder, then, that we experience anger and outrage when watching a national emblem profaned or desecrated. The notion that compatriots desecrating our flag is merely "free speech" demonstrates our propensity to make laws and then carry them blindly to ludicrous extremes: desecrating a flag is "free speech" in exactly the same way that slapping or spitting in the face is free speech ... and the intent is the same.

Like it or not, we use symbols constantly, usually without conscious awareness, and they have the power to affect our behavior more than we realize. Usually the use of symbols is to our benefit because, like words, they are coin-of-the-realm to our thinking processes. But are there any pitfalls or drawbacks associated with their use?

Well, of course there are. You've probably noticed by now that when it comes to human physiology and programming, there are always design flaws and gotcha's. Nothing's perfect. In the case of symbols, there are four possible pitfalls: retaining allegiance to a symbol after it's lost its efficacy; becoming so enamored with the symbolized perfection of a concept that we don't recognize – and hence neglect – real-world less-than-perfect occurrences of the concept; allowing symbols to become stereotypes or caricatures; and forcing real world events into molds they don't really fit.

The derisive term "Battleship Admiral" is a symbol for the danger of maintaining allegiance to a symbol after the concept it represents has lost its efficacy. Superior battleships were long the determinant of superior navies, so admirals lobbied vociferously for more and better. The advent of aircraft capable of sinking battleships changed the equation, but battleships had been the symbol of sea power for so long that most admirals were incapable of recognizing the change – and continued lobbying for more battleships rather than aircraft carriers. Their allegiance to a no-longer-appropriate symbol for sea power dangerously delayed transitioning to a carrier-centric navy.

A second pitfall to our use of symbols is the possibility of becoming so enamored with the symbolized perfection of a concept that we don't recognize – and hence neglect – real-world less-than-perfect occurrences of the concept. Or, put another way, we make a symbol so rigidly stylized that we don't recognize any variations. Once we have in mind that great linebackers or ballerinas have particular physiques, we may deny that a particular linebacker or ballerina is "great" – regardless of his or her performance – if they don't match our "stereotype" of what a great linebacker or ballerina should be.

This brings us to stereotypes and caricatures. A stereotype is "an oversimplified, widely accepted, and typically biased image or description of a group or class of people." In other words, stereotypes are biased symbols of other people, and the bias can be either positive or negative – for them or against them. In the example just described, the stereotype was a positive one – an envisioned ideal linebacker or ballerina. Usually when we speak of stereotypes, however, we have in mind negative or derogatory images of others, perhaps even caricatures. Caricatures are gross distortions of the character and/or characteristics of another person or group, usually for the purpose of mocking them, and often quite vicious. Politics and religion bring out the tribal worst in us and provide the motivations for our more despicable stereotyping and caricaturing of others. Symbolism at its worst.

The final pitfall in our use of symbols is the danger of trying to force real-world events, persons, and groups into existing symbolic "molds" whether they fit or not. Consider writing and trying to publish a book: you will find that publishers have established genres – symbolically named pigeon holes – and your book had better fit neatly into one or they will be incapable of considering it.

The pseudosciences are also particularly vulnerable to this pitfall. Once a sociologic, psychologic, or economic theory – "Behaviorism," "I'm OK, You're OK," "The Laffer Curve" – becomes accepted, not only does its name become a symbol, the theory itself becomes a "symbol" of how to treat the problems it addresses, and its advocates may then see *all* societal, psychological, or economic conditions – appropriate or not – only in terms of that symbolic approach.

• • •

This propensity to develop symbolic concepts and insist that reality conform to them is also discernable in our laws and the creative interpretations we give them. The next chapter, *Law Man*, considers this propensity further.

Chapter 9
Law Man: Man, Not Moses, is the Lawgiver

"Laws control the lesser man; right conduct controls the greater one." – Mark Twain

Moses is not the "Lawgiver"; Man is. Or, more properly, Man is the "Lawmaker."

Human societies everywhere have always made laws, and they always will. We can't help it. Whenever we see social behavior we don't like, we make a law against it. This has been true at least since Man learned to write, for the oldest surviving writings from ancient civilizations contain both snippets and whole bodies of law; the Code of Hammurabi and Torah of Moses are the best-known examples of the latter. It's probable that *all* significant ancient civilizations had written bodies of law, even though not all have survived, and that the written laws were preceded by millennia of oral law.

Perhaps as a child you laid thin paper over a coin, stroked the paper with a soft lead pencil, and marveled at the surprisingly detailed image that emerged of the coin's embossed surface. Similarly, the accumulated history of Man's laws over four millennia provides a "tracing," an overlay revealing much about the underlying nature of Man.

One of the first things revealed is that Man's nature has not changed during those four millennia. The behaviors legislated against when Man first began recording laws have remained remarkably the same in every time, clime, and culture throughout written history: our laws have continuously documented the same propensity for killing, stealing, deceiving, cheating, slandering, and fornicating.

And that is the second thing revealed: the baseness of our nature. Every restrictive law Man has ever made is an acknowledgment that someone has done whatever that law prohibits, and that *we expect Man is likely to do it again unless prevented*. Laws, like bars on a zoo cage, attempt to restrain the animal within: if the animal isn't dangerous, why are the bars needed? Clearly our laws indict us as being, well, the base creatures we are.

A third thing might be inferred from the first two: if Man has been behaving exactly the same way for over four thousand years, isn't that still more prima facie evidence that Man's behavior is programmed?

Besides documenting that we are so undeviatingly deviant that it's quite likely we are wired that way, our overlay of laws also documents that:

- While occasionally self-sacrificing, we are usually self-serving;

- By making things artificially complex, we empower those overseeing the complexity;

- We forget the original intent of our laws and consequently misapply them;

- We begin treating laws we've made as immutable absolutes;

- We make the law into a game played by lawyers and judges.

Let's examine these predilections.

That we are self-serving is clearly reflected in our laws: whether the laws are for a kingdom or a dictatorship, a theocracy or a democracy, they are made up and written down by the dominant groups and inevitably confer favored status upon those groups.

In most ancient civilizations, the king was deemed a god, and the royal court and the priesthood were tightly intertwined. Their laws made no effort to disguise the favored status of the royal family, the priesthood, the aristocracy, and the other upper classes of citizenry because this was assumed to be god-ordained, right, and proper. Thus they prescribed differing penalties for the same crime depending upon who committed the crime and upon whom it was committed: crimes against royal personages and property were severely punished, usually with death, and crimes against slaves were punished only if they damaged the slave's value to the owner. In between, the punishments varied with the social status of the victims and perpetrators.

Such openness is frowned upon today.

For whatever reasons – possibly having to do with improved communications and an increase in the percentage of "educated" people – societies have become less open about their conferring of favored status upon the lawmaking elites. The advent of democratic societies based on the principle of social equality was probably instrumental to this change. Democracies discourage *obvious* favoritism in laws, so as democratic principles became more widely known and the world grew smaller, even dictatorships, oligarchies, and theocracies began making efforts to hide their iron control behind paternalistic verbiage.

Since blatant favoritism isn't acceptable in democracies, a more subtle means of favoring themselves had to be developed by democratic lawmakers. The tendency of laws to become evermore complex – as will be discussed next – provided both the cover and the means. A single innocent-sounding phrase or sentence inserted somewhere within a convoluted law is all it takes to confer favored treatment on some constituency. Thus the favoritism, like the Devil, is in the details, and democracies are awash with lobbyists eagerly trying to get their preferred phrases and sentences imbedded in laws. Lawmakers in democracies continually trade charges and countercharges about who's being more influenced by the competing lobbies.

Making things artificially complex and empowering those overseeing the complexity seem to be programmed inclinations because they are so prevalent: Man characteristically layers useful skills and bodies of knowledge with arcane, complex rules that enable the practitioners to limit access and thus enhance their prestige and economic status. Knowledge is power, and sharing knowledge dilutes the power.

Religions became the earliest practitioners of the artifice of artificial complexity, since their founders' basic teachings were quickly augmented with so many ancillary laws, teachings, doctrines, and interpretations that only a well-trained and certified (sanctified) expert could possibly make sense of them. Just the variety of sources and augmentations alone made their bodies of literature – scripture – complex, particularly since writings in one section often appeared to contradict writings in another. Because it is usually an article of faith in Religion that everything in scripture is true and accurate, the notion of "paradoxes" emerged – generating even more expositions, explanations, and complexity. Thus, no individual alive, no matter how bright, can pick up the scripture from any of the world religions and comprehend its "mysteries" without guidance. They might form opinions, but their opinions would be considered heresies unless approved by those guarding the gateways. It seems that complexity and sanctioned explanations provide more power and job security than even a union. Which is why unions, too, got into the act.

Ancient and medieval craft guilds led the way. As unique fields of craftsmanship, artisanship, and artistry emerged in societies, bodies of knowledge essential to their practice began to accrue. Naturally, whenever craftsmen developed a skill or technique enabling them to produce a superior product, they wanted to keep it a trade secret if possible. Even without economists, humans are adept at recognizing the relationship between supply, demand, and how much they get paid. Thus the stratagem of artificially limiting the availability of a product to increase its value also came naturally ... long before Capitalism. While the ruling classes were pioneering monopolies, the working classes were pioneering trade unions. Not having the option of staging a strike and surviving, they instead created artificial complexities for entering a trade and becoming privy to its secrets – kind of like the Religions. Thus they achieved the noble goal of maintaining a high-quality product, and also gained the ability to influence prices (by controlling the number of practitioners) and to enjoy the power and prestige of being guardians of their gateways.

If you're thinking the same sort of behavior – artificial complexity and restriction of membership to limit supply –

can also be seen in the "professions," well, I think you may be right. Actually, medical, legal, and academic practitioners began employing these techniques right alongside the religious practitioners – well before craftsmen were sufficiently emancipated to follow suit. Today our modern professional societies are regularly described as being "unions" that have a stated noble goal of maintaining quality but also unstated goals of maintaining high salaries (by limiting their numbers) and protecting members from outside discipline.

Probably the only profession not having a de facto union is the "oldest profession," and that's only because it's not legal in most places. If it ever becomes widely legalized in the United States, expect to see an ACA (American Courtesan Association), higher prices, and a thorough crackdown on unsanctioned providers.

Our tendency to make things artificially complex – and empower those overseeing the complexity – is embarrassingly evident in our legal systems. The Judeo/Anglo/American notion that law decisions must be based on previous decisions unadulterated by common sense – even when all previous cases had differing circumstances – guarantees tortuous logic and strained reasoning. It causes law decisions to constantly "branch out" from base decisions in order to adapt to changing times and circumstances unforeseen by the lawmakers. Over time, "The Law" becomes a thicket of intertwined, overlapping, often contradictory decisions roamed by armies of sophists seeking the most advantageous ones to invoke. Inevitably, such a "legal system" degenerates into a game played by lawyers and judges – those who tie the blindfold over the eyes of Justice and tilt the scales. The ideal that the purpose of courts of law is to administer justice routinely gets elbowed aside in the zeal to apply abstractions cleverly enough to circumvent justice. Is it any wonder Shakespeare included the throw-away line, "The first thing we do, let's kill all the lawyers," or that Dickens had a character say, "If the law supposes that ... the law is an ass, an idiot"?

Part of the problem is that once laws are written, the concerns and conditions prompting them are forgotten, leaving them open to misapplications never intended or envisioned. The danger of this happening could be reduced if all laws had a "spirit of the law" codicil describing why the law was written, what it was intended to accomplish, and what it was not. Such codicils don't exist, of course. Shouldn't we make a law requiring them?

Another part of the problem is our tendency to treat established laws as absolutes and to apply them blindly, even grotesquely, ignoring the human plights involved and that justice was once the goal. "We're sorry; we can see it isn't really fair or just in this case, but it's the Law, so we can't do anything about it. ... Too bad." ... Yeah.

This brings us to the final thing our skein of laws reveals about us – we make a game of the law and consequently become complicit in crime: throwing out clear evidence because it was "improperly" or "illegally" attained, or releasing the guilty because of "procedural errors," is nothing less than becoming accessories after the fact. If evidence is improperly or illegally attained, censor or charge those acquiring it, but don't discard the evidence as though it doesn't exist; if police or prosecutors don't follow procedures properly, again, censor or charge them, but don't release the criminal. People's lives and well-being are at stake: making the law a blind rule-enforcement game and forgetting that justice (Justice!) is the goal makes criminals of the game players ... and those who consent.

• • •

In summary: What we see played out in the Law arena is but another instance of the human dilemma played out in all human arenas. We are flawed, some think fatally. We reach for the skies, but somehow remain mired in mud. We seek justice for all, but find that laws cannot be written so finely that they address all possible circumstances and motivations – the time always comes when enforcing a law blindly, as it is written, will result in grievous injustice. Thus we need wise, honest, and compassionate judges not bound to the letter of the law to discern truth and rule justly in spite of inadequate laws. Unfortunately, wise, honest, and compassionate judges do not endure as an institution; the temptation to side with the rich and powerful in order to become rich and powerful, or with the ideological elite in order to be fawned upon, inevitably erodes justice. Even when wise, honest, and compassionate judges are found, their successors are seldom so for long.

Thus we fall back on our pitifully inadequate laws. We proudly proclaim: *"Ours is a nation of laws. We are ruled by laws, not men,"* never realizing this is an admission of failure. The ideal is a nation of wise, honest, and compassionate people, and it's because we aren't wise, honest, and compassionate for very long that we accede to flawed laws administered by flawed people. We accept injustice as our due; we're probably right.

• • •

Now that we've discussed our lawmaking prowess, what better to discuss next than the prowess that spawns an embarrassingly large percentage of our lawmaking – and lawbreaking. The next chapter is, of course, *Sexual Man*.

Chapter 10
Sexual Man: Starving for Pleasure

"What would men be without women?
Scarce, sir, mighty scarce." – Mark Twain

In a now famous 1954 experiment, electrical probes were inserted into the "pleasure area" of the brains of laboratory rats to enable them to give themselves a jolt of "pleasure" whenever they wanted by pressing a pedal; they also could press another pedal whenever they wanted to give themselves a dose of food. The experimenters found that the rats pressed the "pleasure" pedal repeatedly – thousands of times an hour – even while starving to death from lack of food. When the experiment was repeated with monkeys, the monkeys fared no better.

How would humans fare in such an experiment?

Since medical ethics preclude experimenting with human beings, we have to content ourselves with merely musing about the possible outcome of so fiendish an experiment. A more answerable question to consider is whether there's any evidence in the real-world laboratory of human experience to suggest we might, in some lesser way, "starve" ourselves of useful things in order to "pleasure" ourselves with things that provide nothing beyond transient pleasure itself. Given our species-long fascination with Sex, the fact that Sex provides the greatest natural pleasure jolt known to Man, and that Sex notoriously spawns a whole menagerie of irrational behavior, the question clearly deserves to be examined further.

And we shall.

But first we need to review what's known – and unknown – about human sexuality in general. In what ways are we sexually like other animals, and in what ways are we different? Are we basically monogamous or polygamous? Are our sexual "taboos" learned or instinctive? Do we have hardwired mating rituals, softwired social rituals, both, or neither? Is homosexuality natural? Are fetishes natural? Are some sexual conventions and lifestyles right, proper, and healthy, while others are wrong, improper, and unhealthy? And finally, do we as individuals or societies allow the allure of sexual pleasures to distract us from more meaningful – even essential – pursuits?

The answer to the first question, "In what ways are we sexually like and unlike other animals?" is far reaching, and affects the answers to the remaining questions. It seems that sexually, humans are truly unique among animals. While we have all the basic hardwired animal programming for copulation – and end up using it – we also incorporate firmwired and softwired components that we rely upon to override our hardwired impulses. Only humans are capable of this because only humans have language and the subsequent abilities to consciously think, to store softwired ideas, and to promote ideas to firmwired beliefs. Thus we are the only animals that can take conscious control of our sexual activities and *choose* to be sexual celibates, hedonists, or anything in between.

Key to that control is another uniquely human endowment: we do not have to rely upon estrus – periodic female sexual heat – to trigger sexual interest, but are physically capable of sex at almost anytime after puberty. The only other species approaching this capability is the Bonobo chimpanzee, and these primates do so not by freeing sexual capability from the bonds of estrus, but by having estrus last nearly the entire menstrual cycle. Being able to have sex most of the time and unable to ignore the triggering stimuli, Bonobos *must* intermingle sex play and intercourse with practically all of their social activities. Since they're also the only other primate that engages in face-to-face intercourse and oral sex, this makes for interesting watching at the zoo, but it's clearly counterproductive for animals wanting their lives to have more meaning than that scripted by hardwired behavior. Bonobos demonstrate what we might be like if we *didn't* override our hardwired sex drive with firmwired and softwired restraints.

The tension between our hardwired programming and the firmwired/softwired programming modifying it shows up repeatedly whenever we attempt to answer any of the major questions about our sexual behavior. Apparently, it is not only normal but *necessary* for human societies to place cultural restrictions upon sexual behavior. There is not now, and probably never has been, any human society that has given carte blanche to sexual licentiousness. While the intriguing carvings in the temples of Ankor Wat raise the possibility that their civilization may have been an exception to this rule, it's more likely the Bonobo-like behavior depicted there was the privilege of only a ruling or priestly caste.

In all civilizations having written laws, ancient or modern, the sexual behaviors permitted and forbidden are inevitably spelled out in minute detail. The details differ from civilization to civilization and society to society, since each culture has had to resolve the conflict between hardwired urges (for sexual licentiousness) and softwired urges (for a stable society) in its own way. Programmers would refer to this process as "Finding a software solution for a hardware problem."

Because so many different "solutions" to the human sexual conflict have been tried by so many different cultures over so many millennia, it's possible to recommend almost any form of sexual behavior and be able to point to some culture, at some time, as being an enlightened example of that behavior. Hedonists, ascetics, and in-betweens never quite agree on which culture to emulate, however, so the debate goes on.

As of this writing, no authoritative studies have been published cataloging *Homo sapiens'* predominant sexual schemas and how societies have fared using them. Doing so is ... difficult ... since history doesn't conduct controlled experiments, and societies usually prosper or fail due to hopelessly entangled factors. Some useful data may eventually be gleaned from the Scandinavian (and some European) countries' recent experimenting with different sexual schemas, but its usefulness will be limited because: 1) different addictive drug schemas are also being tried, and that muddies the results; 2) the countries are sheltered by the Pax Americana, so any weaknesses induced by their experimenting won't become obvious until they must contend for survival on their own.

In the absence of hard data, we are free – compelled, actually – to make up pronouncements about what sexual schema best benefits human society based upon our existing biases toward hedonism or asceticism, and our existing understanding of human nature. Thus, what

follows reflects my particular understanding and biases ...
but it's as honest as honest effort can make it.

• • •

We've thus far addressed only one question, "In what
ways are we sexually like and different from other
animals?" Still to be considered are: Are we basically
monogamous or polygamous? Are our sexual "taboos"
learned or instinctive? Do we have hardwired mating
rituals, softwired social rituals, both, or neither? Is
homosexuality natural? Are fetishes natural? Are some
sexual conventions and lifestyles right, proper, and
healthy, while others are wrong, improper, and unhealthy?
And finally, do we as individuals or societies allow the
allure of sexual pleasure to distract us from more
meaningful – even essential – pursuits?

• • •

Are we basically monogamous or polygamous?

It is generally surmised that humans evolved away
from dependence upon estrus so human parents could bond
in rewarding, long-lasting monogamous relationships to
better raise children. This can't be proved, nor can it be
disproved, but we're compelled by our nature to make up
explanations for things unknown, and this is as reasonable
a "working hypothesis" as any.

The problem is that throughout our history we've
allowed so many breaches of and exceptions to the rule of
monogamy that it's sometimes questioned whether we
really *are* monogamous. It was once thought that
copulation in other monogamous species was purely
monogamous, so perhaps our many exceptions meant we
weren't truly monogamous. It's now known that other
monogamous animals also have more exceptions to the

rule of monogamy than was first observed, so our numerous indiscretions needn't disqualify us.

It's also now known that there *might* be a biological basis for monogamy and polygamy. It seems there are two nearly identical species of voles – small, Midwestern, mouse-like rodents – that differ primarily in that one is social and monogamous, and the other asocial and polygamous. By inducing small gene-based changes to their brains, researchers have been able to cause the latter to behave like the former. The changes to the brain aren't dramatic, just an alteration in the distribution pattern of hormone receptors, but the change affects when the "pleasure" neurotransmitter dopamine is released, apparently allowing a jolt of pleasure to be associated with the first sexual partner and to cause the vole to become, well, "addicted" to that first partner. Since we share much the same brain chemistry as other mammals, it's possible our monogamous/polygamous behavior, too, might be governed by gene-based receptor distribution patterns. Should this prove to be true, our varying degrees of adherence to monogamy could be attributed to varying receptor distribution patterns among people ... and those who have said, "Love is an addiction," will have been closer to the truth than realized.

Such a scenario would also explain our historical susceptibility to love triangles and fatal romances – to having harmless flings unexpectedly turn into tragicomedies when the "addiction" or "bonding" factor suddenly kicks in, inappropriately, for one or both of the participants. The commonness and the humanness of this occurrence – not to mention the havoc it creates – are attested to by the millennia of literature and drama portraying endless variations on the theme. So it is sorely tempting to treat this possibility as fact, but I remind you, it is still speculation.

• • •

Are our sexual "taboos" learned or instinctive?

As described in Chapter 1, *Programmed Man*, anthropologists attest that taboos against incest – sexual intercourse between near blood relatives – are present in all human cultures, demonstrating they are indeed instinctive – wired-in. But the chapter also acknowledged there are many *cultural* taboos – pseudo-taboos – that differ from culture to culture and thus permit drawing the conclusion that all taboos except those against incest are cultural and arbitrary. Some have indeed drawn that conclusion and gone on to proclaim that all other so-called sexual taboos are learned, and that the only reasons for cultural rules against sexual promiscuity are practical concerns about pregnancy and disease. Emphatically, they say no instincts are involved.

That conclusion and its corollaries are themselves arbitrary, and suspect. Despite the wide variety of sexual schemas human societies have tried, there seems to be at least three characteristics constant enough to be considered as probably having instinctive origins:
- cultural restraints on sexual behavior
- resistance to childhood sexual exploitation
- reluctance and embarrassment to talk about Sex

• *Cultural restraints on sexual behavior*

As already noted, human societies do not give carte blanche to sexual licentiousness: they may differ markedly on what the restraints are, but there are always restraints. Possibly the reason "this is not only normal but necessary" is that it is instinctive – that we are programmed to do so for the same reason we are programmed to care for and not harm tribemates: to avoid behavior harmful to the society.

- *Resistance to childhood sexual exploitation*

The currently prevailing notion that early guilt feelings about sex are simply the result of being scolded or shamed for asking innocent questions is possibly true – but it's also possibly false. Children who are sexually abused by persuasion rather than force often feel lingering guilt despite strong reassurances that they were innocent victims. Why? ... Well, if they had experienced twinges telling them, "This is wrong," but allowed stronger twinges of fascination and curiosity to overcome them, that would explain their inability to feel complete innocence – internally they would "know they knew." Whether such an inborn instinct exists isn't known, but the possibility shouldn't be discarded without consideration.

- *Reluctance and embarrassment to talk about Sex*

The broader notion that all guilt feelings (and consequent embarrassment) are the result of cultural conditioning is also unproven. Anthropologists have found that cultures around the world evidence not only a common reluctance and embarrassment to talk about Sex but also a common means for dealing with it – remarkably similar coarse and ribald humor. Details differ due to differing sexual schemas, but the overall tone and "purpose" – to reduce embarrassment – is the same. If our reluctance and embarrassment to talk about Sex as freely as we do any other subject is the result of cultural conditioning, then it's remarkable that all human cultures, everywhere, have coincidentally chosen to impose exactly the same social restrictions on speech.

• • •

Do we have hardwired mating rituals, softwired social rituals, both, or neither?

Did our escape from the bonds of estrus also free us from mating rituals? It's difficult to say. Because of our ability to override most of our hardwired sexual programming with firmwired and softwired social programming – with customs – it's currently impossible to tell where one leaves off and the other begins.

As stated above, we clearly have the basic hardwired animal programming for copulation – and end up using it – but how we get from meeting to mating has always varied widely depending upon the society and the circumstances within it. Western societies have generally avoided polygamous, women-as-property schemas and adopted instead monogamous schemas with varying degrees of fidelity. Within such societies we consistently evolve some series of approved steps – spoken and unspoken social rules – to guide and govern the meeting-to-mating process. The duration and formality of this "courting" or "dating" process varies widely – even wildly – in differing societies and differing times. It ranges from strait-laced Victorian to "anything goes," and the degree of community and family involvement ranges from absolute to none. Regardless of the process, our hardwired programming eventually gets its chance to perform – ideally, at the end of the process, but not necessarily.

What about individual behavior? When community norms permit potential mating partners freedom to interact, do humans exhibit any hardwired programming leading toward copulation? Well, yes we do ... quite a bit in fact. And we begin rehearsing our "moves" quite early in childhood, long before they're needed – ask any observant grade school teacher. Our inherent body and facial "languages" often speak louder than words, and we're wired to "read" and interpret them unconsciously. Actors and actresses make their livings by "speaking" with body and facial language as well as with words, and mimes speak eloquently with only body language.

Watch television commercials for only a short while, and you can begin to catalog our sexual "invitation to the dance" postures and glances. Marketing firms make fortunes utilizing those attention-getting postures and glances to seduce us into remembering and eventually buying their clients' products. And when someone comparing artistic nudity to pornography says, "I know the difference when I see it," they're telling the truth. Our unconscious programming sorts out all the subtle signs and signals, and renders a sure verdict whether what we're seeing is innocent or provocative. ... We know.

The cosmetic industry is also well aware of our susceptibility to visual sexual cues. It's well documented that from time immemorial, females – and often males – of our species have doctored their appearance to exaggerate the features we're programmed to respond to as sexually attractive. Drawings from ancient Egypt show them pioneering creative cosmetic techniques that can't be improved upon today, and incidentally also document their awareness that high heels serendipitously make female tops and bottoms more pleasingly prominent.

And then there's this quote from circa 740 BCE:

... the daughters ... are haughty and walk with outstretched necks, glancing wantonly with their eyes, mincing as they go, tinkling with their feet ... the finery of their anklets, their headbands, their crescents ... their pendants, their bracelets, and their scarves ... their headdresses, their armlets, their sashes, their perfume boxes, and their amulets ... their signet rings and nose rings ... their festal robes, their mantles, their

*cloaks, and their handbags; their garments of gauze,
their linen garments, their turbans, and their veils.*

The inclination of human females to enhance their sexual attractiveness clearly did not go unnoticed by this perceptive observer – Isaiah the Prophet.

Before summarizing what all of this says about human "mating rituals," we should also consider the possibility that human sexual behavior, like many other mammals' sexual behavior, might be influenced by pheromones – odorless chemical molecules released by one member of a species to affect other members. Although odorless, pheromones are detected by an organ in the nose that works in parallel with the more familiar olfactory system that detects odors. It was long thought that humans had only a nonfunctioning vestigial remnant of that organ, but it's now known that, although ours is simple compared to other mammals', it is functional and can demonstrably affect a few "somewhat" sex-related biological processes, like synchronizing the menstrual cycles of women. Despite heroic efforts by perfume and medical companies to discover some "aphrodisiac" pheromone that would make the bearer more attractive to the opposite sex, there is no evidence to date that pheromones affect human sexual behavior.

As an aside, it's interesting that we *welcome* the possibility of unconscious brain processes triggered by pheromones controlling our sexual behavior but *resist* the notion of unconscious brain processes controlling our other behavior. This demonstrates, once again, how selective we are in examining evidence: we welcome what flatters or pleases us, and ignore or reject the rest.

Whether or not any of the foregoing demonstrates human "mating rituals" is in the eye of the beholder, or in this case, the mind of the Reader – You. If you're predisposed to see humans as having mating rituals, you will undoubtedly interpret this material as supporting that view; and if you're predisposed to see humans as not having mating rituals, you will equally undoubtedly interpret this material as refuting that view. Regardless, for convenience I am going to refer to it as a "mating ritual" when making the following observations:

- The human mating ritual is normally spread out over time rather than occurring as a single continuous act. (Obvious exceptions are rape, which is hardwired animalistic behavior, and "one-night stands," which occur when societal conventions break down, are weak, or are foiled by circumstance.)

- Women are as active in the ritual as men: their conscious and unconscious efforts to be attractive and to attract a desirable partner are as necessary as the efforts of the men who pursue and preen for them. (The alternative view would be that humans are the only sexually dimorphic species existent where the females are objects of a mating ritual rather than participants.)

- Firmwired and softwired cultural programming – customs – impose particular forms upon the ritual in differing cultures.

- A new environment apparently can trick our instincts, our programming, our mating ritual into starting over: "Hey, in this environment I'm still single." Hence, office romances, traveling salesmen with girls in every town, and sailors with girls in every port.

● ● ●

Is homosexuality natural?
The answer is "Yes" ... but with a footnote.

It is "Yes," in that natural development in the womb results in a statistical percentage of people having a sexual attraction for members of the same sex ... but the footnote points out that the statistical percentage is the result of design flaws in a very complex process, and was not "intended" to occur. If the process worked perfectly, there would be no homosexuality: the genetic sex dictated by our chromosomes would be correctly reflected in our genitalia and in the brain structures governing our male/female thinking, feeling, and behaving.

But this is not the case.

The development of genitalia and brain structures matching the genetic sex depend upon the secretion and detection of particular hormones at particular times during the process, and this sometimes fails. The manner and degree to which it fails can vary, so there is also a variance in the results: it is possible that genitalia, thinking, feeling, and behavior might all be affected in differing degrees depending upon which hormonal secretion/detection sequence failed.

Variations of the genitalia from the genetic code can be observed and often resolved surgically; variations of the brain structures cannot. Although some male/female brain structural differences are gradually becoming known and detectable in brain scans, doing anything to alter them is impossible. Thus there is a wide range of "homosexual" behavior, from quiet and loving committed couples, to flaunting and taunting profligates. Given all of this, how should homosexuals be treated by the rest of society?

In a rational and ideal world, such a question would be considered as ridiculous as asking how Pennsylvanians should be treated in Ohio: "Why, the same as Ohioans, of course." But in the real world, we are not rational; we have competing sexual schemas to contend with, and we are handicapped with religious doctrines formulated before the cause of homosexuality was known.

If a sexual schema that strongly encouraged monogamy and strongly discouraged public sexual display were predominant, it is possible the problem would resolve itself: faced with known facts and such a schema, religious leaders could conclude that their historical strictures against homosexuality were actually against the associated rampant promiscuity and public disorder, and they could begin to stress the need for faithfulness in all unions. Without such a schema in place, however, it isn't possible to welcome the quiet and loving committed couples without "welcoming" the aggressive and confrontational profligates as well. Those believing that sexual licentiousness is harmless to a society have no problem with this, but those believing that it is harmful ... do.

• • •

Are fetishes natural?

We do not yet know what causes some humans to become pedophiles, or to require particular clothing, objects, or settings to become sexually aroused. We do know that some birds can be induced to develop sexual fetishes for objects if they're exposed to them at a critical developmental period, but there is no evidence of this occurring in humans – except for the striking parallels in behavior. Because the parallels *are* so striking, however, it would be wise to leave open the possibility that we, too, may in some still unknown way be subject to "bonding" with objects or circumstances at critical periods in our sexual development. If such were the case, it would explain this otherwise inexplicable behavior.

Are sexual fetishes, then, "natural"? Can we apply the same arguments as with homosexuality and say they're natural but due to some "design flaw" in the developmental process? No, we can't. Or, at least, we shouldn't. Doing so requires hypothesizing – making up – not only a process similar to that observed in birds but, in addition, making up "flaws" in the imagined process. As yet, there isn't even any research data to show how brain processes cause fetishes in birds, let alone in Man. Pseudoscientists have no problem heaping speculation upon speculation with straight faces, but it's not a practice to emulate. Wondering aloud whether human fetishes might arise in the same way as bird fetishes is sufficient to get us stoned. ... Let's leave it at that.

• • •

Are some sexual conventions and lifestyles right, proper, and healthy, while others are wrong, improper, and unhealthy?

On this question, not only are "experts" divided but so is most of the Western world. The question has become a battleground issue fiercely fought over by competing political tribes, and – as taught in Chapter 3, *Biased Man* – beliefs that are opposed tend to become extreme and polarized. As a consequence, whether "alternate lifestyles" are healthy or not can no more be discussed rationally than can abortion – which is actually a subset of the larger argument. Generally, the sexual-lifestyle stance you favor is decided by the relative importance you place on three competing desires:

- A desire for sexual pleasure
- A desire to avoid consequences – diseases and unwanted pregnancies
- A desire for a stable society

If you are a true believer in a political party or a religion, it's probable that the weight you place on these competing desires is determined for you by the tribal tenets of your party or religion.

Regardless, our desire for sexual pleasure always has and always will be in conflict with our desire to suffer no unwanted consequences and our desire to have a stable society. Consequently, there always have been and always will be two ongoing debates: How do we resolve the conflict between our desire for sexual pleasure and our desire to not suffer consequences? And how do we resolve the conflict between our desire for sexual pleasure and our desire for a stable society? The positions we take in these two ongoing debates effectively determine whether we will conclude a given lifestyle is "healthy" or "unhealthy."

In the first debate there is some hard evidence to consider, so it conceivably could be resolved, but in the second debate hard evidence is difficult to impossible to come by, so it may be a permanent feature of human societies. The second debate will be discussed in the next section because examining the tradeoff between sexual pleasure and a stable society is actually addressing this chapter's main concern: do we as individuals or societies allow the allure of sexual pleasures to distract us from more meaningful – even essential – pursuits?

In the first debate, how to resolve the conflict between our desire for sexual pleasure and our desire to not suffer consequences, the hard evidence is this: sexual conventions and lifestyles likely to cause unwanted pregnancies and spread sexually transmitted diseases, particularly the dread AIDS, are *measurably* less healthy than those that do not; we have copious, irrefutable statistics. But even this *provable* evidence is regularly discounted with claims that proper education and proper use of prophylactics minimize or eliminate the dangers. As usual, we simply brush aside any data contrary to what we dearly want to be true. The possibility that our endgame copulation programming, hardwired and irrational, might be too powerful to be easily and often interrupted with rational thought is simply ignored. After all, we *are* rational, aren't we? Suggesting that in the heat of action we might irrationally discard protection simply because it was jeopardizing a satisfactory completion, how silly. ... How human.

When obvious and demonstrable evidence that some lifestyles are harmful can be cavalierly rejected, what chance do less provable claims have? Once giddy with the notion of endless guiltless sexual pleasure with no consequences, we'll renounce heaven and earth, not to mention logic and reason, to attain it. Thus, we argue in one breath that Man's sexual drive is too powerful to be thwarted – "You can't expect young people to not have sex" – and in the next breath we argue that it's easily managed by our reason. Similarly, despite millennia of restraining our hardwired sexual programming with every imaginable variety of softwired/firmwired restraints, suddenly it's "unnatural" and "unhealthy" to do so. This, in spite of evidence (as recent as the much mocked "1950s") that sexual schemas discouraging casual and promiscuous "recreational" sex can be accepted as easily and naturally as any other schema. We now portray such schemas as unenlightened and unbearable burdens. In our current "wisdom" we somehow argue that because sexual restraints can't eliminate all sexual transgressions, we should eliminate all sexual restraints! ... Logic is not Man's strong suit.

In light of our remarkable ability to ignore obvious evidence when it's inconvenient, what chance do you think unprovable, circumstantial, and anecdotal evidence will have in the sexual pleasure vs. social stability debate?

• • •

Do we as individuals or societies allow the allure of
sexual pleasure to distract us from more meaningful
– even essential – pursuits?

Except for periods of imposed peace – Pax Romanas
and Pax Americanas – human tribes and societies are in a
constant struggle with other tribes and societies to survive:
in the best of times the struggles are cultural; in the worst
of times, war. Although we like to imagine that peace is
normal, history devastatingly demonstrates that "peace" is
only the interlude before the next war. It shouldn't be that
way, but because of the way we're wired – our hardwired
animal natures – that's the way it is.

We're also engaged in another constant struggle: the
struggle for our existence, our lives, to have meaning.
Whenever our struggle against other tribes allows, even in
its throes, we strive for wisdom, knowledge, and
understanding ... to rise above warring, and to instead
raise Truth and Beauty ... Science and Art ... our
justifications and our glory.

These two epic struggles, one to exist, the other to be
meaningful – one driven by hardwired programming, the
other by softwired – contend with each other throughout
time, and constitute the human dilemma. Should we
content ourselves to merely be, or should we discontent
ourselves to be ... more? The outcome of this struggle has
ever been in doubt, and ever will be. It seems Armageddon
is here and now ... forever.

Enter Sex, stage right, sometimes tiptoeing on little cat
feet, sometimes sloshing in great muddy boots. What role
does Sex – the sexual schema adopted by a society – play
in helping or hindering the society's struggle to exist and
to be meaningful? Again, do we ever "starve" ourselves of
needful things in favor of transient pleasure? Can a

society's preoccupation with Sex as an end in itself harm the society, or is it a harmless pursuit?

Since there's no "proof" for either position, we differ mightily in our answers: if we are hedonists, and our hardwired programming is only lightly fettered with softwired restraints, we'll gleefully join in the chorus calling for more sexual "freedom"; if we are ascetics, and our hardwired programming is tightly tethered by softwired restraints, we'll dolefully decry any Sex beyond procreation – and that reluctantly; if we're somewhere in between ... we'll insist on something in between.

This is because, as you've come to realize, existing beliefs bias our thinking and blind us to evidence contradicting them. Thus we can – and regularly do – simply wave aside evidence against anything we currently believe and devoutly want to be true. In past centuries we discounted the notion that unseen microbes could cause diseases, and in this century we as easily discount the notion that promiscuous sex can harm societies. "You can't prove it," we smirk and breezily ignore the significant circumstantial and anecdotal evidence that decadent societies become prey for others. We can do this because circumstantial and anecdotal data is not scientific and "proves" nothing. For the data to be useful, it would have to allow comparing societal data from periods of strict sexual mores with data from periods of loose sexual mores – with all other factors being the same: we could then make pronouncements about which schema was "better" based on how the societies subsequently fared. Since history doesn't provide such controlled data, the circumstantial and anecdotal evidence "proves" nothing, and we can happily believe whatever we want. Thus this debate is destined to remain a permanent part of human societies.

The knowledge that our behaviors are largely programmed, however, does provide one additional argument. While we have the ability to override our hardwired sexual programming with softwired schemas, it is not an infinite and isolated ability; our sexual programming still has to interact with our other tribal programming, and it's reasonable to expect that some schemas contribute better than others to the overall health and strength of the tribe. Schemas based on committed sexual fidelity have been predominant throughout our history and are clearly "safe," whereas schemas based on sexual promiscuity have no significant track record and do have circumstantial evidence warning against them. Why then would any rational person favor the latter over the former?

Sadly, you know the answer. Man is not rational.

So *my* answer to this chapter's question is, "Yes, whenever those advocating sexual promiscuity predominate, we can and do starve ourselves of needful things in favor of transient pleasures." ... But I can't prove it.

• • •

To recap and rephrase the major contentions made by *Sexual Man*:

- Sex is "intended" to bind mates for life as well as to produce children; unfortunately, its success rate at bonding isn't too great, so augmentation with softwired/firmwired programming – some sexual "schema" – is required.

- Sex provides the greatest natural physical pleasure humans experience, but it's ephemeral and has no lasting benefit when used for anything other than bonding and procreation.

- Circumstantial and anecdotal evidence suggests – but cannot prove – that widespread promiscuous sex destabilizes a society, making it weak within and vulnerable without.

- Human societies will irrationally succumb to the lure of hardwired sexual licentiousness whenever their softwired/firmwired sexual schemas do not override it.

● ● ●

Slipping into preoccupation with promiscuous sex is but one of the ways a society can degenerate and become vulnerable. The next chapter, *Degenerate Man*, examines two others.

Chapter 11
Degenerate Man: The Twofold Path to Destruction

"The more things are forbidden, the more popular they become." – Mark Twain

Given our binary nature, it isn't surprising that Man has evolved two opposing ways to degenerate: first, by continually eroding the softwired controls we place on our hardwired animal nature; and second, by hardening our softwired controls into inflexible dogma – Hedonism vs. Pharisaism. The ditch to the left or the ditch to the right – which ditch do you fear the most?

Let's look first at human societies' tendency to degenerate through Hedonism.

All human societies have rules of behavior – rules of what can and can't be said, shown, or done without censure or punishment: making rules to govern behavior is as natural to us as forming tribes. Thus it's particularly perverse that *breaking* those rules seems as natural to us as *making* them. It appears there is something in Man's nature that does not like restrictions: no matter how minimal and reasonable a society's rules, there are always groups wanting to bend or break them, and no matter how low a society sets the bar of acceptable behavior, there is always pressure to lower the bar one more notch ... one more notch ... just one more notch.

Why? ... Why do human societies build up codes of acceptable behavior, only to dismantle them one restriction at a time? Our human nature doesn't fluctuate – it's a constant – so why are our standards of behavior constantly in flux? Why do we cycle between Puritanism and permissiveness, and never settle upon enduring standards?

Part of the answer is known, since we are now aware that irrational behavior persistent throughout our existence is undoubtedly caused by our subconscious programming. We do not yet know, however, the nature of the subconscious "subprograms" whose interactions somehow result in our cyclic behavior pattern. Once again, all we can do is hypothesize.

One reasonable hypothesis is that the built-in struggle between our instincts and our ideals – our hardwired and softwired programming – is a major factor. This struggle is so omnipresent that it's difficult to address any aspect of human nature and behavior without encountering it. It seems to have become a theme in this book without any conscious intent to make it so.

Any enlightenment, any improvement in Man's estate through improved understanding of Man's nature, necessarily results in restricting some of our natural – that is, animal – behavior, and the animal within inevitably resents the restrictions and begins to chip away at them. We can't admit to ourselves that we're lowering the bar to patronize our base instincts, so our Great Explainer function provides rationalizations – excuses:

- *We are restoring freedom by throwing off the shackles of Blue Laws ... of Prohibition ... of Censorship ... of whatever – that were ignorantly imposed by Neanderthals ... Philistines ... Puritans.*

* *We have more knowledge than preceding generations, so the social rules inherited from them no longer apply; our greater understanding enables us to now do safely the things they found hazardous.*

* *We are righting the "inequities" between social groups by granting underprivileged groups the same behavioral rights as privileged groups.*

The excuses are laudable – that's their purpose – but they're also hopelessly flawed by the underlying assumption that we are rational.

Consider the excuse that we're *"restoring freedom" by discarding restrictive laws that were needlessly imposed by the "unenlightened."* This excuse is doubly flawed: first, by the already mentioned assumption that we are rational, and second, by the assumption that those "imposing" the laws were "unenlightened."

Thanks to our ability to automatically react with negative emotion and unconsciously generate self-convincing arguments against anything opposing our firmwired beliefs or hardwired desires, we easily convince ourselves that those sponsoring laws we find "restrictive" are misguided, unenlightened, mean-spirited, and just plain dumb – even if "They" were earlier generations of "Us." If we were rational and wanted to treat our predecessors fairly, we would examine the circumstances at the time the restrictive laws were passed, determine what behavior concerned them, and give honest consideration to the possibility that removing the restrictions would allow the return of such behavior. Since we're driven by our instincts rather than our reason, however, we don't do that.

If by any chance we did, and discovered there were good reasons for passing the laws and that they were motivated by good intentions rather than bad, we still wouldn't be stuck with the laws ... because we could then invoke the second excuse, *"Our greater knowledge enables us to safely do things that were previously harmful."* This excuse is a step up from the first, for it at least acknowledges that some past behaviors *were* harmful and needed restraint, but it then goes on to imagine that our greater knowledge will now allow us to do them safely. The reality is that no matter how great our knowledge, we will *never* be able to safely do things that have historically brought us grief. Our human weaknesses are immutable: the only way we can "control" them is by fostering social environments – softwired programming – that rein them in. Whether past, present, or future, whenever we imagine we can indulge our weaknesses and that our reason will keep us from harm ... we come to harm.

The third excuse used to lower the bar of acceptable behavior without admitting we're doing so, is that we're simply *"righting inequities between social groups"* by granting underprivileged groups the same behavioral rights as privileged groups. Since privileged groups have the means to disregard inconvenient social restrictions – they can get abortions when they're illegal, and liquor when it's prohibited – "righting inequities" translates into either requiring the wealthy, influential, and powerful to be more ascetic, or allowing the rest of society to become more hedonistic. Guess which happens? Reform movements strong enough to enforce social mores on the wealthy, influential, and powerful are exceedingly rare, so inexorably the bar gets lowered.

Besides the built-in tension between our hardwired and softwired programming, a second hypothesis for our cycling between Puritanism and permissiveness might be our impulse to form subtribes and seek power by subverting the dominant tribe's tenets. Since tribes dominate by imposing their beliefs – and thus rules and laws – breaking rules and laws is a way to exert independence – to declare oneself a freeman rather than a vassal of those making the laws. Thus the first act of any group seeing itself as an emerging – and, of course, superior – subtribe is to publicly break the dress and decorum codes of the dominant tribe. Almost any rule or law can be dismissed as "arbitrary" and "burdensome," so whenever a subgroup wants to challenge the status quo, it has no difficulty finding *something* objectionable to use as a cause – particularly since dominant tribes tend to become bureaucratic and self-serving, and to spawn reams of arbitrary and burdensome laws. Unfortunately, in the joy and heat of rebellion, no thought can be given to which of the standards being overthrown *are* arbitrary and dispensable, and which might be wise and essential to the society's wellbeing ... so often the good is thrown out with the bad, and standards deteriorate.

A third hypothesis for degenerating standards might be the time-honored profit motive: there is much money to be made pandering to our hardwired animal instincts. Give us a whiff of whatever our weaknesses are, and we'll gladly, repeatedly hand over our money for the slimmest chance, the slightest hope of having our weaknesses gratified. With fortunes to be made catering to human weaknesses, it's inevitable there will always be lobbying to lower the bar on what's allowed by society, just one more notch. The Sex, Gambling, and Entertainment "industries" have vested interests in lowering restrictions on what is allowed, and since we *like* being titillated, teased, and taken, we object but little and pretend to believe their lobbyists' claims that they're simply providing innocent, healthy, community services that do society little harm. ... We can't let the bluenoses run our lives, can we?

Which, of course, brings us to the second way that societies degenerate: by hardening their rules into inflexible dogma zealously controlled by the dominant tribe. Such doctrinal-sclerosis is often "mothered" by the fear that deteriorating standards are destroying the society, and "fathered" by the belief that imposing rigid adherence to rules is the way to save it – or it may just evolve as a dominant tribe succeeds in becoming more and more ... dominating.

Historically – and still today – the most visible examples of such societies are ones based on religions – that's why Western societies use names like "Pharisaism" and "Puritanism" to describe them. It seems that whenever a religion's founder dies, his followers inevitably metamorphose his teachings into doctrines, dogmas, and rituals that can't be questioned; whenever a society's religious leaders also control the government, the society's laws equally inevitably harden into inflexible dogma.

As you should be aware by now, it is not *religious* beliefs but beliefs *per se* that trigger such behavior. And being aware of that, you probably would expect to discover similar behavior when only *secular* beliefs are involved. You would be right. Secular societies are as susceptible to hardening rules into inflexible dogma as are religious societies. One example is the so-called "politically correct" phenomenon already described in Chapter 7, *Storytelling Man*: when a political party's tenets prevail long enough, or if traumatic events imprint them, they become "accepted truth" and cannot be questioned without inviting outrage and derision – the same as if they were religious dogma.

Similarly, the phenomenon of a religious leader's teachings becoming dogmatized can also be seen when a renowned and revered *secular* innovator dies: his followers formalize his teachings into a methodology, and create a "school" where serious people guard, defend, and disseminate it. These "schools" effectively become mini secular-religions. The fields concerned with human behavior – the pseudosciences – demonstrate this the most, although even the hard sciences aren't immune. Thus the Aristotles and Platos, the Freuds and Jungs, the Meads and Skinners, all have received posthumous near-deification by their awe-struck followers, and their edited teachings become "gospels" not to be questioned.

It is demonstrable that once inspired teachings, religious or secular, become owned and maintained by institutions, even the most enlightened of them degenerate into dogma and self-serving addenda. As a consequence, all human tribes – governments, religions, political parties, unions, professions, what have you – eventually become institutionalized and self-serving, and their entrenched dogmatism provides justification for those seeking to tear them down.

• • •

It would appear, then, that Man is doomed. Whenever a modicum of enlightenment is achieved, it becomes hardened into dogma and paves the way for those resisting enlightenment to tear it down ... one notch at a time. The image of Sisyphus in Hades, doomed to forever push a boulder up a mountain only to have it forever roll back to the bottom, is an appropriate metaphor for Man. Hence the ebb and flow, the waxing and waning between sense and nonsense, between Wisdom and its degenerate twin nemeses – Hedonism and Puritanism. Can anything break this cycle, or will it become our death spiral?

I hold out only faint hope: it is *possible* that we may have programmed within us an instinct capable of surmounting our self-serving and self-destructive compulsions. If you enjoy irony, you'll be grimly amused to learn that it's the same instinct supposed to spawn our many bloody religious wars: our spiritual instinct. The next chapter, *Spiritual Man*, examines that possibility.

Chapter 12
Spiritual Man: Beyond Mud-Daubed Idols

"Kindness is the language which the deaf can hear and the blind can see." – Mark Twain

The notion that in the past, Religion was based on ignorance and superstition, and we are now "beyond that" is wrong on both counts. The only difference between our ancestors and us is the data we have to work with: they were just as intelligent, believing, and/or skeptical as us, no more, no less. There has always been a mix of those professing belief in religious doctrines and those questioning them, and the breakdown has seldom been based on intelligence or education. Much to the chagrin – and frustration – of those doing the questioning, there have always been highly intelligent and educated people who, nonetheless, were "Believers." The illogic of believing things that can't be proven has never been a handicap to us.

Since the Enlightenment, however, those questioning Religion have invoked Science as their ally and become severe in their assessment of Religion: thus if you consider yourself enlightened and scientific today, you may well contend that Religion is not only a primitive superstition unworthy of modern Man but also a pestilence – a polluting source of dissension, war, and ignorance that should be wiped from the face of the Earth and the history of Mankind forever.

If you are enlightened and scientific, however, you must also admit that your contention is based upon the axiom – the underlying assumption – that Man is *rational*, and that this axiom has now proven false. Consequently, being enlightened and scientific, you must admit that when an axiom is proven false, all of its corollaries – all of the conclusions based upon it – have to be tossed out and rethought starting with a better axiom.

That is what we are about to do. We are going to reexamine Religion based on the truer axiom that "Man is not rational, but is programmed by instincts to behave the way he does." In the process, we'll examine:

- Are *religious* tribal tenets the cause of war and dissension, or tribal tenets themselves?

- Why is Religion more susceptible to human flaws than Science?

- Does knowledge of our underlying nature alter the "Science vs. Religion" debate?

- Is part of our underlying nature a "spiritual" instinct that is a progenitor of religions?

- Could such a spiritual instinct provide hope for overcoming our self-destructive behavior?

Are religious tribal tenets the cause of war and dissension, or tribal tenets themselves?

That this question still needs to be asked and answered is a tribute to the power our beliefs have over us, and to how difficult it is to dislodge a belief even when it's proven false. The answer was written in blood across the face of the Earth decades ago, when atheist Communism swept across a third of the world and slaughtered more millions in the name of secular beliefs than Religions had in the name of religious beliefs.

Not only did Communism demonstrate that we kill as willingly for secular beliefs as for religious beliefs, it also demonstrated that secular beliefs warp our behavior in exactly the same way as religious beliefs: Religion is notorious for subverting Science whenever scientific facts do not reinforce religious doctrines, and Communism proved equally adept at subverting Science whenever scientific facts did not reinforce Party doctrines.

The most famous example of this occurred when Trofim Lysenko, a minimally trained but politically correct biologist, was elevated to head the Academy of Agricultural Sciences of the Soviet Union. The ensuing scientific debacle – which gave birth to the term, "Lysenkoism" – became one of Soviet Communism's many reenactments of the Spanish Inquisition, with Lysenko starring as Torquemada. He systematically denounced all of the Soviet biologists who wouldn't support his colorful but misguided agricultural theories, and eventually all were imprisoned, exiled, or executed at the hands of the Soviet secret police. Nikolai Vavilov, Russia's best-known biologist and cofounder of the science of genetics, died in prison, and genetics in Soviet Russia died with him for a full generation – at an incalculable cost to Soviet agriculture and the Soviet people. Religious beliefs couldn't have done it better ... or differently.

The calamitous arrival of Communism in human history should have triggered a reevaluation of the thesis that Religion is the primary cause of human strife, but in the centuries since the Enlightenment, that thesis itself had become a belief – and thus impervious to reason. Despite the clear evidence provided by Communism, many still cling to the notion that it is *religious* beliefs – and therefore Religions – that are the source of Man's woes, rather than *tribal* beliefs and tribal ways. Religion has effectively become a scapegoat for those unwilling to face the unflattering reality of our nature: that we war because we are tribal, territorial animals; that we treat beliefs as if they were territory; that we subjugate others by imposing our beliefs upon them; ... *and that it doesn't matter at all whether the beliefs are secular or religious.*

Prior to the event of Communism, of course, the beliefs obstructing scientific progress were blatantly religious. When Religion was supreme and Science newborn, Religion attempted to kill Science in its cradle; when Science grew and gained power following the Enlightenment, it returned the favor ... and humans have been doing so in its name ever since. If we were rational, this might arguably be a good thing, but we now know humans are *not* rational, so the Science vs. Religion controversy needs to be reexamined in the light of this knowledge.

Why is Religion more susceptible to human flaws than Science?

Since Science and Religion are both run by the same species – Us – it would be surprising if one demonstrated flaws traceable to our human programming and the other did not ... but that appears to be the case: Science is intellectually in good repute, and Religion is intellectually in poor repute. So let's review some of the recognized faults (sins?) of Religion, and examine whether Science is indeed immune to them ... or if it's just a matter of degree and circumstance.

The most glaring sin of Religion, of course, is its rampant tribalism. Maps of medieval Europe revealed a crazy patchwork of feuding tribal fiefdoms, and modern Christianity seems to have matched and surpassed that. Every tribe of Christendom has its own cherished traditions and doctrines, and no intent whatsoever of giving up a "jot or a tittle" of any of them ... which is peculiar behavior for a religion whose founder encouraged followers "to be one, that the World might believe." It should warn us how difficult it is to overcome our wired-in tribal behavior ... even to save our souls.

A second sin of Religion, alluded to above, is its impulse to suppress or discredit discoveries about the physical world that don't mesh with dogma. The best-known example is the 17th Century Inquisition trial where, to save his life, Galileo had to renounce Copernicus' discovery that the Earth revolved around the Sun. Today, no single authoritative religion has the power to outlaw or suppress scientific findings, but the fervor with which some religious groups oppose (for example) the teaching of Evolution in high schools makes it plain that they would happily exercise that power if they could. This compulsion, we now know, is a flaw of our nature: we are wired to discount, discard, and destroy evidence contrary to our existing beliefs.

A third sin of Religion is the habit of promoting scriptural texts and derived doctrines to "absolutes" that replace and thwart the spiritual truths underlying the scripture. The periodic attempts of religious reformers to overcome this habit inevitably fail because it seems we are predisposed to prefer idealized absolutes to wrestling with whether the circumstances and intent of scriptural texts are actually applicable to the current circumstances. And if you note that this behavior is similar to that of Lawyers and Judges who place the letter of the law above the spirit of the law ... you are right.

We are wired to promote ideas "generally true" to beliefs "absolutely true," and to thereafter treat them as settled, unquestionable, and widely applicable to circumstances never originally envisioned. Hence bumper stickers like, "God said it, I believe it, that settles it." This frequent forgetting of the spiritual truths underlying doctrine undermines Religion's attempts to influence society: instead of quoting the "wheat" in scripture that teaches self-sacrifice and caring for others, we more often quote the "weeds" that allow self-righteousness and tribalism.

A final noteworthy sin of Religion, of course, is hypocrisy. That the pulpits and pews of churches are often occupied by pastors and parishioners who preach against lying, but lie; against stealing, but steal; and against seduction, but seduce, is no longer even denied: the evidence is too ... evident. The sad truth is that our softwired altruistic programming is always vulnerable to being overridden by our hardwired base instincts. While there are few joys greater than pointing and laughing at culprits who were recently lecturing us, nonetheless, there is no evidence that religious altruistic programming is more prone to failure than secular altruistic programming. It's just that Religion's "preachiness" makes it much more delightful when a prince or pauper of the Church falls.

These, then, are the major flaws of Religion: *Tribalism; Suppression of dissenting ideas; Promotion of partial truths to unquestionable absolutes; and Hypocrisy.* They should sound familiar, because they are all basic flaws of our human nature, shown in Chapters 1 through 4 to be directly traceable to our species programming. So why do the corridors and laboratories of Science not display these flaws as clearly and colorfully as the cloisters and naves of Religion? Is Science somehow immune to our human nature? Are people of Science less irrational than others?

Unfortunately, no; but, fortunately, the milieu of Science is immensely less vulnerable to human flaws than the milieu of Religion. The primary reason is that tribes don't naturally incorporate "a science" into their tribal beliefs as they do "a religion," so when tribes fight and try to impose their beliefs on one another, it isn't in the name of their science, but in the name of their religion.

A second reason is that the Scientific Method, the "confessional" of Science, requires rigorous testing of theories (i.e., beliefs) before accepting them – a practice that is impractical to incorporate into Religion because religious beliefs are generally impossible to test.

A third and final reason the Scientific milieu is less vulnerable to human flaws is that relatively few people have a vested interest in a particular scientific theory being True, but most people have a vested interest in a particular religion or view of religion being True. Nonetheless, in spite of Science's vastly more favorable milieu, human flaws are still discernable there. ... They just aren't as obvious. So let's examine the "flaws of Religion" as they appear in Science:

Tribalism

Tribalism isn't as obvious within Science as within Religion because religions must go head-to-head fighting for the same territory, but sciences are more like peers whose territories do not overlap: biology doesn't have to compete with chemistry, which doesn't have to compete with physics, which doesn't have to compete with mathematics, and so on. Tribalism *does* show up in Science, however, whenever there are competing theories within the same field ... and then it is often as fierce and irrational as between religions. It is not uncommon to find cadres of scientists not speaking to one another, and employing the academic equivalent of trash talk in their articles and letters-to-the-editors in technical journals.

Suppression of dissenting ideas

Similarly, the suppression of dissenting ideas isn't as obvious within Science as within Religion because it occurs mostly within scientific fields rather than between them. Even when there are competing theories within a field, the onus of the Scientific Method usually overcomes the human impulse to maliciously suppress disagreeable thought – particularly when no one theory enjoys overwhelming support. This all changes, however, when the third human flaw – the promotion of partial truths to unquestionable absolutes – comes into play.

Promotion of partial truths to absolutes

This occurs when a favored but only partially proven theory is assumed by everyone in the field to be true – then the Scientific Method is forgotten, the theory is prematurely promoted to unquestioned fact, and any contrary evidence is airily dismissed. Even in Science our hardwired programming can override our softwired programming, and once an idea becomes accepted as truth, it requires an inordinate amount of evidence to refute it. The landscape of Science is littered with such occurrences. Some examples are:

• A century or so ago it was noted that, yes, there was a resemblance between the east coast of the Americas and the west coast of Europe and Africa, but any suggestion that the two may have once been joined was ridiculed as unscientific nonsense. Decades of growing evidence that corresponding points on the two coasts had similar geological, archaeological, and biological features were ignored because they didn't fit the prevailing theory; it wasn't until studies of the mid-ocean ridges made it impossible to ignore the data any longer that the Plate-Tectonic theory of intercontinental drift was finally accepted as scientifically valid.

- Mere decades ago, if you believed that acupuncture provided any medical benefit other than psychosomatic relief for uneducated and superstitious people, you would have been laughed out of the medical community; any evidence that its effects were real, and that it might actually be of benefit was routinely ignored or derided, and discarded. Today acupuncture is accepted as a legitimate medical procedure, even though it's still not fully understood.

- Similarly, decades ago, tribal "medicine men" were dismissed as primitive quacks relying on superstition and ignorance rather than having useful knowledge that benefited their tribes. Today major drug corporations send out teams to track down and interview the remaining medicine men and women, hoping to learn about medicinal plants they can analyze to come up with new drugs.

- As described in Chapter 1, when Behaviorism ruled the scientific community, it was believed that humans were born as "blank slates" and that all our behavior was the result of being "conditioned" by experiences and subsequent feedback. Science trudged down this wrong road for several generations, bowling over dissenters and airily dismissing contrary evidence. Behaviorism's defenders fought with the fury of true believers, and succumbed to the evidence only after a long drawn-out battle. Amazingly, pockets of Behaviorism still exist in academia.

- Also still alive and well today is the acute fear of anthropomorphism described in the Introduction: "Anyone remotely suggesting a 'human-like' quality in the behavior of a lesser animal is subject to such ridicule that his best bet is to seek another line of work. It simply isn't admissible that as Man ascended the evolutionary path, he may well have retained many of the 'lower-animal' mechanisms and layered his new abilities atop them, and that consequently it's quite likely some 'human-like' behavior will be observed in lower animals because it's really 'lower-animal' behavior retained in us." Nonetheless, anti-anthropomorphism still dominates much of the scientific landscape.

Hypocrisy

And finally, what of Hypocrisy – the remaining of the four major flaws of Religion? Does Science, too, suffer from hypocrisy, or is it somehow immune?   Unfortunately it is not. As we have just seen, the hypocrisy of Science is that it professes a creed demanding that hypotheses be tested before being accepted, but nonetheless regularly embraces conclusions not yet proven based on the conviction – the sincere belief – that, well, they soon will be. Some in the scientific disciplines have even graduated into reverse superstition – into believing with insufficient evidence that things not explainable by current theories are not "unknown" but are "false" and should be rejected with as much fanfare as possible. Science, too, is conducted by human beings with human failings, and only the limiting circumstances make Man's flaws less devastating in Science than in Religion: even when guided by a creed that demands the testing of hypotheses before accepting them, Man still falls into the trap of conjuring up whole worlds from a grain of sand, and biasing subsequent observations to bolster the worlds envisioned.

The failings of Religion are timeworn and well known; the hope of Science is still so fresh that its failure to address many of our needs goes unnoticed and ignored. Believers in Science need to learn that many of the things taught by Religion – even though not understood – accurately portray the reality of human nature and address innate human needs: the enduring religious teachings are not arbitrary rules made up to maintain power, but are truths distilled from centuries of experimenting in the human laboratory with what works and what doesn't.

Does knowledge of our underlying nature alter the "Science vs. Religion" debate?

Yes it does ... but not dramatically.

That Religion and its supporters have historically overstepped their bounds is well known, but now we must acknowledge that Science and its supporters, too, have sometimes overstepped theirs by unscientifically rejecting almost all religious teachings rather than only provably false ones. Delighted by the new wonders it was discovering following the Enlightenment – physical causes for many things previously attributed to God's direct intervention – some in Science extrapolated its findings to conclude that all things would eventually be traced to simple cause and effect in a purely mechanical world. Irreligious people (as opposed to merely enthusiastic scientists) adopted this hypothesis and promoted it as if it were proven, smug in the assumption that future scientific discoveries would continue to verify it.

The gap between Science and Religion widened when the Behaviorist "blank-slate" theory, mentioned above, was introduced. Early studies with newborn babies failed to detect any instincts except suckling, body functions, crying, and expressions of fear when lowered suddenly as if falling, so the theory was generally accepted as scientifically true. Those opposing Religion proclaimed this proved there was no religious instinct – no "word of God written on Man's heart" – and that for Religion to disappear it was only necessary to stop teaching it. Subsequent studies, of course, have demonstrated that Man is indeed programmed with a multitude of instincts, and the Communist experiment demonstrated that the religious instinct is not easily eradicated. Nonetheless, those who see Religion as the root of all evil continue to believe Science is their ally and that for people to be "educated," "intelligent," and "enlightened," Religion must be shunned.

Ironically, Science has advanced so far – particularly in the fields of physics, astronomy, and mathematics – that it now takes more faith for a layman to believe Science's teachings than Religion's. What are we ordinary people to think of a Creation that began with the entire universe somehow packed into a microscopic dot: a universe that's now awash with mysterious dark matter and dark energy, colossal "dark hole" cosmic whirlpools that suck up anything passing too close, and a physical reality that fades, not into electrons, protons, and neutrons as it once did, but into a mystical realm of probability populated by charmed particles, quarks, and ten – no, make that eleven now – dimensional "superstrings"? If that's "Truth," it certainly is stranger than fiction. In comparison, "Chosen People," "Triune Gods," and Reincarnation seem benign and comforting. ... The "mysteries" of Science have exceeded the "mysteries" of God!

This is not to say that the weirdness claimed by Science isn't true – only to state the obvious: for anyone but the relatively few scientists actually working in these advanced fields, believing the teachings of Science today requires more faith than believing the teachings of Religion. We laypeople can no more understand the esoteric universes hinted at by detritus in mathematical scientific formulae than we can understand the arcane jargon and twisted logic of theologians. Once we drift off into subparticles or into more than three dimensions of space, we are forced to accept the teachings of Science entirely on trust and faith: that we do so is not because white coats are better than black robes for enhancing credulity, but because the reputation of Science hasn't been tarnished by several millennia of genocidal tribes claiming they had the only true science.

Is part of our underlying nature a "spiritual" instinct that is a progenitor of religions?

The evidence that Man has a powerful "spiritual" instinct – a predisposition to believe in a creating, guiding God (or gods) – that manifests itself in the form of religions is overwhelming: Carl Jung included "God" as one of the archetypes in the "collective unconscious" of Mankind because of the sweeping anthropological evidence that all human cultures have embodied some concept of "God" ... and the power of the instinct was dramatically demonstrated by the failure of the Soviet Union to eliminate religion despite seventy years of the cruelest efforts.

These facts should not be discarded lightly. If you find yourself doing so, it is probably evidence that you already possess or are possessed by a belief that religion is unscientific, evil, or both. That's hardly to your shame, because religion clearly is *not* scientific and historically *has* been used for evil – many times. The fact that an instinct results in unscientific behavior and is frequently used for evil, however, is not a good and sufficient reason to deny its existence: the behavior resulting from our sexual instinct is hardly scientific, is frequently used for evil, and yet few suggest denying its existence.

Curious, isn't it? We have these two pervasive, wired-in instincts, and while only a sprinkling of ascetics ever recommend ignoring our sexual instinct, large segments of societies regularly clamor to ignore our spiritual instinct – usually when it proves inconvenient to their sexual instinct. The two instincts influence human behavior in strikingly different ways, vaguely analogous to the way two of Nature's forces affect the physical world: the strong nuclear force attracts subatomic particles powerfully at very close range, but has no effect on larger objects or at longer ranges; the gravitational force affects particles and small objects insignificantly at any range, but controls the motion of large objects, even at great ranges.

Our sexual instinct, like the strong nuclear force, is powerful, but its "range" is short; while it affects individual relationships powerfully, it is not normally a factor affecting the course of events in a society or in history. In contrast, our spiritual instinct is comparatively weak in its effect on individual relationships, but can pervade a society and dominate the course of events. Exempting the Helen of Troy myth, our sexual instinct does not usually lead to wars and social upheavals, while our spiritual instinct – manifested in religions – frequently does.

This is why many people have come to view Religion as harmful, even evil.

Which in turn is why the notion that our spiritual instinct may be the only means of saving us from ourselves is ... quixotic. Nonetheless, there are persuasive reasons to advance such a theory.

Does our spiritual instinct provide hope for overcoming our self-destructive behavior?

We now know our self-destructive behavior results from our species programming – our hardwired tribal, territorial-animal programming – and that there is no means of changing that programming. Even if at some time in the future it becomes possible to modify human behavior through genetic engineering, we'd still encounter the Catch-22 described in Chapter 5, *Idea Man*: world peace and cooperation is a *prerequisite* for behavior-modifying genetic engineering; otherwise, "good" tribes would be producing pacifists, and "bad" tribes would be producing superior warriors bent on killing them. Breeding pacifists may be a good thing, but without world peace it's suicidal. The question thus becomes, "Is it possible to achieve lasting world peace *while still tribal, territorial animals programmed to war with one another?*"

Two factors allow the answer to this question to be: "Yes, it is possible, but barely so." The two factors are our hardwired trait of love and sacrifice for tribal members, and our capacity to override hardwired programming with softwired programming that has been promoted to firmwired beliefs.

The hardwired trait of love and sacrifice for tribal members has been our saving grace throughout our existence: although we murder, maim, and rape members of other tribes with guiltless animal abandon, we are wired to care for members of our own tribes, so within our tribes we create beliefs and laws to cage our animal impulses. The ancient law codes of the Babylonians, Israelites, et al, bear witness to this, as do our modern law codes: all codify our innate instinct to care for and not harm tribemates, and to punish or shun offenders.

The second factor – our capacity to override hardwired programming with softwired programming that has been promoted to firmwired beliefs – is probably the mechanism through which we "create beliefs and laws to cage our animal impulses" within tribes. From what we know about the human brain's functioning, we can piece together a theory of how this might work: Chapter 2, *Deluded Man*, showed that – thanks to neuroscientists' work with split-brain patients – it is known that our brain's Great Explainer function automatically generates explanations for any unexpected action, and that those explanations have the certitude of beliefs; Chapter 3, *Biased Man*, noted that the Great Explainer function also kicks in to generate explanations for unexpected emotions – for feelings. Thus, in response to a "felt" hardwired impulse to care for and protect tribemates, our Great Explainer automatically generates explanations with the impact of beliefs to justify the impulse. Species-wide, throughout our history, we always have and always will generate similar beliefs (and subsequent laws) codifying our hardwired impulse to care for and not harm tribemates.

We do not have any such hardwired impulse to care for members of other tribes. In fact, we have a hardwired impulse to dominate or destroy them, which is why we have never "Just lived in peace." So we ask, "Is it possible for all the major national tribes of the world to come to see themselves primarily as members of one single overarching human tribe, so our instinct for intra-tribal caring and cooperation can become operative rather than our instinct for inter-tribal domination?" ... That is, of course, what we have meant when we've asked throughout our existence, "Can't we all just live in peace?"

And throughout our existence the grim answer has always been, "No, not with logic, not with reason, not with intellectual abstractions."

Now that we know Man is not rational, this begins to make sense.

Now that we know Man is not rational, we realize that to achieve our ends we have to work *through* our wired-in programming, not in opposition to it. We have to find some way to "program" ourselves – majorities in all the major nations of the world – with firmwired beliefs capable of overriding our impulse to war.

Theoretically, it is possible that secular beliefs could be used for the task – since all beliefs have the power to control us – but spiritual beliefs clearly are tailored for the task: they have been at work controlling our animal urges *within* tribes ever since we evolved, and they demonstrate a numinous power not found in secular beliefs. The spiritual instinct from which they arise is a true instinct – present in all human tribes, everywhere – and has demonstrated throughout history that it has the capability to change the minds and behavior of men; it apparently predisposes us to exploit spiritual beliefs to control our behavior.

Another recommendation for spiritual beliefs is that all of the major world religions already have teachings within them, somewhere, that encourage their followers to see others as themselves ... to see Mankind as one. Granted, the teachings aren't always prominent – they're sometimes buried in seldom-read sections, and they're usually ignored in favor of teachings that portray the religion as superior – but nonetheless the good teachings are there, and provide the "seeds" for religions to reform themselves ... if they ever become aware of the critical need to reform.

Consider: Our spiritual instinct isn't an instinct for a particular religion, but an instinct to be good to our tribemates – an instinct for "goodness." In response to the felt impulses stemming from this instinct, our Great Explainer generates explanations that embody some form of a "Spirit for Goodness," and they become part of our tribal religions. As with everything else, our tribal nature hardens our tribal religions into particular forms and corrupts them with self-serving teachings. Each religion becomes like a clay idol that, instead of being decorated with pieces of colored glass, is decorated with "doctrines" and "sacraments," so each has its own unique outward appearance and its own unique collection of dogma. But beneath the mud-daubed surfaces of them all, remains that glowing Spirit for Goodness ... and its message shines out through the cracks as the "good" teachings within our religions. Those teachings together form an overlay, an outline of our instinctive image of God and Goodness, and provide a template for what "perfect" Man should be. If ever Man is to be "saved" from himself, it will have to be through these teachings, elevated to the world-wide religion of a single tribe, Mankind.

This spiritual, altruistic idea that Man's individual and collective purpose is to achieve Goodness – to become as loving and caring across tribal boundaries as within tribal boundaries – provides the only hope that Man will not eventually destroy itself. Realistically, only Religion can spread this idea and elevate it to a firmwired, behavior-controlling belief. But until religions, all religions, reform themselves and begin caring more for Goodness than for dogma, doctrines, and rituals ... there really is no hope. So, if you imagine yourself to feel any love or concern for Mankind, labor for the reform of Religion – not its destruction.

• • •

The next and final chapter, *Evolving Man*, summarizes what we have learned about our nature, and considers the likelihood of Mankind ever evolving to a sufficiently higher level of understanding and behavior to ... finally ... live in peace.

Chapter 13
Evolving Man: The Task Before Us

"Apparently there is nothing that cannot happen today."
– Mark Twain

Now you know more about human nature than any generation before you ... ever.

Now, more and more, you will understand the human behavior you observe, and more and more you will recognize our species' tribal programming controlling nearly every aspect of our lives, even while we remain convinced we are in control and have rational reasons for our irrational behavior. And, more and more, you will find yourself ruefully acknowledging, "Once you realize Man is not rational, things begin to make sense."

But it may take a while.

Human nature being what it is, you will initially observe self-serving tribal behavior only in *other* tribes, particularly your scapegoat enemies, and you will vehemently deny that similar behavior exists in your own. Even when undeniable evidence is presented, you will still angrily deny it in every possible way your Great Explainer can generate. Only with the greatest effort will you eventually accept that, yes, even *your* tribes – noble causes and all – harbor the same tribal flaws as all the other tribes because we're all in bondage to the same tribal traits. They permeate our existence and predispose us to blindly and angrily defend tribal beliefs, to caricature and scapegoat tribal opponents, to feel no empathy or sympathy for members of opposing tribes, to blindly support tribe members when they harm outsiders, and whenever possible to dominate other tribes and impose our beliefs upon them. The evidence that we *do* behave this way is everywhere and would overwhelm us were it not for the power of our brain's Great Explainer function to deceive us into believing we have sound, rational reasons for our irrational behavior.

Recall these words from the *Introduction*:

"The biggest obstacle to improving the human race can easily be identified: it is **You and I, and our existing beliefs***. We come equipped with a certitude that we and our groups – national, political, religious, philosophical, whatever – are not part of the problem, but that all competing groups are, and if they would only cooperate with Us, peace would reign. That, as you will see, is the way we're wired to feel and believe; we can't help it."*

You could not understand the truth of those words then ... but you can now.

Samuel L. Clemens – the great Mark Twain – wasn't fooled: he saw through both his own Great Explainer and that of others; he harpooned and lampooned human behavior mightily, and labored to shame it into reform. He didn't succeed, of course – he couldn't – and ended in frustration, grief, and tears. His painful insight that Man's persistent problems were not anomalies but part and parcel of "the *Damned* Human Race" has now been vindicated: the universal human behavior that he observed, marveled at, and lamented is finally fully understandable – in terms of our "hidden programming" – in terms of "The Tribal Programming Theory of Human Behavior."

The *Introduction* also proclaimed, *"We're now approaching a turning point in human history, the point at which Mankind finally acquires sufficient understanding of its own nature to begin diminishing its self-destructive behavior."*

But we have barely reached this "epochal moment in time," and we have barely begun to discern our true nature. You who are reading this are among the first to become aware not only of the nature of the problem but of its enormity. You are among the first to become aware that Mankind's eternal question has been irrevocably changed from: *"WHY can't we all just live in peace?"* to: *"Given that we are programmed to contend and war with one another, HOW can we live in peace?"*

How, indeed! The remainder of this chapter, and this book, addresses that new question.

• • •

Chapter 12, *Spiritual Man*, summarized the new awareness that we can never escape our hardwired instincts, but that it is possible to override them with softwired ideas promoted to behavior-controlling firmwired beliefs; we have also become aware that the "seed" ideas necessary to begin the process are:

1) Our innate tribal programming is the cause of human conflict.
2) Human conflict can be lessened only if:
   • We understand our hardwired tribal programming and its consequences;

- We modify our controllable programming –
  teachings – accordingly;
- We grow to believe the truth of these teachings –
  that they are essential for our survival – so
  strongly that they become behavior-controlling
  beliefs.

The problem, of course, is that "We" means all the major nations and religions of the world must share this understanding and participate in the effort. If even one nation remains unrepentant and uncooperative, the others cannot proceed to develop workable war-avoiding accords and disarm – and all the dictatorships, oligarchies, theocracies, and semi-democracies of the world dependent upon the status quo will scorn the effort and sabotage it. Even true democracies may be so riddled with corruption and political infighting that they become incapable of agreeing on anything, even striving to achieve world peace.

As of this writing, none of the nations of the world, none of the "think tanks" and influential academic bodies, and none of the world religions are even aware of the human programming that has condemned us to war in the past and will continue to condemn us to war in the future. It will take generations for awareness of our bondage to war to become acknowledged worldwide, and more generations for the gruesome reality to sink in sufficiently for all the nations to agree, "We really ought to do something about this." In the meantime, it can only be hoped that a benign democracy like the United States remains sufficiently powerful to keep the world from falling under the domination of a less benign power, one whose only concept of world peace is world dominion. Clearly, sadly, there will be no end to wars in our time or for generations to come: we will continue to plead, "Peace,

peace!" but find ourselves either at war or preparing for war.

This is not a welcome reality: we are tempted to refute it with the willful delusion that Man is capable of overcoming his hardwired animal nature *with reason alone*, and to scapegoat any who claim otherwise. With our Great Explainer's help, we can easily dismiss the age-old evidence that Man has never succeeded in doing so, and the new-age evidence that it stems from unchangeable programming, and live on in the "bliss" of ignorance, denial, and flat-Earths. ... Resist that temptation. ... The Age of Aquarius has come and gone, Armageddon is now and forever, and the New Day Coming in the Morning will only reveal the same war-littered landscapes as all our yesterdays.

Isn't it time for the *Damned* Human Race to grow up?

You ..., I ..., We ..., cannot save the human race. Its salvation clearly requires that *all the nations of the world* recognize, believe, and teach that we are born predisposed to war, and that *all the nations of the world* cooperate in programming ourselves with beliefs strong enough to avoid it. If that miraculous day ever comes, it might *then* be possible to implement protocols and disarm, but until then there will *never* be world peace. The sad reality is that a United Nations composed of unenlightened national tribes with only a few seeking world peace and the rest seeking advantage is inherently – systemically – incapable of achieving and maintaining peace. This is not opinion: it has been demonstrated repeatedly. Yes, the United Nations is better than nothing, and, yes, it is better to work within it, but do *not* delude yourself about the natures and dispositions of the nations and their rulers. ... They, too, are members of the human race.

Also, do not delude yourself with the notion that all tribes, all nations, all religions, are equally "valid" and that none is "better" than others. That notion merely demonstrates once again our propensity to run logically amok – to extrapolate an idea to the extreme, make it an absolute, and become possessed by it. Contrary to the notion, not only do "Good" and "Evil" exist in human affairs, they are measurable: Good arises from our instinct to support and care for tribemates, and Evil arises from our instinct to dominate and destroy others. Whether tribes are "Good" or "Evil" is measurable by how they treat minorities within, and to what degree they tolerate and cooperate with rivals without. Tribes and nations that repress and brutalize their minorities and aggressively seek world domination are simply … Evil. The only sense in which national, ethnic, and religious tribes are "equal" is that they all have the same *potential* for both Good and Evil; what they actually *are* is determined by their operative programming, and is measured by their actions.

As acknowledged, we cannot save the human race … but we can nonetheless work toward that goal by choosing to be less a part of the problem. If we do not, if we choose to remain comfortable within our tribes and ignore the murderous consequences of our tribal programming, we are assenting to and participating in the ongoing inhumanity of Man to Man. Or, as Mark Twain put it, we are not only marching in the procession, we are carrying a banner.

No, we cannot save the human race, but we can vow to be less a part of the problem. Long-lasting seminal changes for the better can occur when new truths are spread over time by many individuals throughout many tribes and eventually become accepted as being a "better way." Religions have often spread in this way, as did the

Enlightenment. Thus for tribes and the world to *eventually* change, it will have to begin with individuals within the world's many tribes introducing and spreading the new truths, the "New Enlightenment."

If you have come to accept the reality of human tribal programming and want to lessen its control over you, there are steps you can take. The necessary first step is learning to detect and compensate for the effects of your subconscious "Great Explainer." Whenever you experience a surge of annoyance, anger, or rage at something someone says, that is a sign your Great Explainer has kicked in and is goading you to strike ... to defend a tribal belief and self-righteously destroy the attacker. Remind yourself that the Great Explainer is dedicated to reinforcing your existing beliefs, has no concern at all for either truth or consistency, and is an incredibly convincing liar. The rebuttal arguments it automatically generates will frequently be illogical, inconsistent, and even farfetched, but you will nonetheless feel absolutely certain they are true. ... Distrust them.

Once you learn to recognize and compensate for the biasing effect of the Great Explainer, you will begin to realize your own tribes' tenets cannot be the whole truth, even though you think they are. You will remember that once we become aware of and concerned about dangers in one direction, the Great Explainer causes us to automatically reject warnings of danger in the opposite direction – and to invent malicious and nefarious motives for those who raise such warnings. To overcome this, rather than dismissing your opponents' concerns and arguments arbitrarily, discipline yourself to listen to them and to understand them sufficiently to be able to summarize them ... accurately.

If you do so, you will find yourself less eager and willing to stereotype and caricature your tribes' scapegoat enemies. You will remind yourself that once we come to regard an opposing group as "the enemy" we unconsciously start to view all of them as being like the worst of them, that we become predisposed to interpret everything they do and say in the worst possible way, and that we extend to them none of the leeway, slack, or understanding we do our friends.

As you progress in this pilgrimage of understanding, of enlightenment, you will find yourself more frequently considering the "greater good" as well as your tribes' self-interests. You will notice we are predisposed to choose the actions and options most favorable to us, even when they are harmful to the commonweal, and that our Great Explainer easily convinces us our behavior is not only justified but somehow noble. You will observe that we are forever tempted to impose our desires whenever we have the power to do so, and to ignore the long-term divisive effects – the ill will – we create. To counter this, you will begin committing yourself to the practice of building consensuses that recognize the concerns of all, even when your group has the power to dominate.

Through all of this you will be developing principles – ideas you believe in so strongly you are willing to impose them not just upon other tribes but upon yourself, your own tribes, and your tribal leaders. You will be becoming … honest.

● ● ●

If only this envisioned scenario were easy … and unopposed.

The tribes you belong to effectively control what you say and do because along with membership came the tacit agreement to adopt their tribal beliefs as your own – or at least to appear to do so. You *need* tribes within which to function, but the more powerful and influential a tribe is, the less it tolerates members calling for moderation. Your resolve to be less a part of the problem will be sorely tested, for to promote reasonableness, fairness, and moderation within your tribes will require you to go against the grain of both instinct and tribal peer pressure, and no matter how gently you proceed, you risk being shunned as an apostate or as a traitor to the noble cause. You will probably be able to persist only if you become possessed by the belief that the long-term survival of your tribes and the human race *depends* upon the new knowledge being disseminated and acted upon.

... So, once again, we encounter the theme that has surfaced repeatedly throughout this book – the theme of an eternal struggle between our hardwired instincts and our softwired ideals/firmwired beliefs – a struggle that conjures up the image of a titanic cosmic battle, and takes on a quasi-religious aura even when the beliefs aren't overtly religious.

• • •

We come now to the end of this treatise.

I promised in the *Introduction*: "If you have the fortitude and tenacity to read this through, it will explain to you much about yourself because it will explain much about the human race ..."

I believe I have fulfilled that promise. I believe you now know much more about yourself and the human race than when you started. And I *hope* you have begun to realize that the biggest obstacle to Man's evolving toward peace is *not* the perennial Evil tribes but the inability of the rest of us to understand ourselves sufficiently to end our own warring and cooperate in preventing Evil leaders and their followers from becoming ascendant. As long as we prove unwilling or incapable of reforming ourselves and our own tribes, what chance will we have of reforming others – and what right?

The lesson is clear: To work toward world peace, we must first understand our tribal nature and work toward cooperation with the tribes we oppose – the political, religious, and secular groups we *think* are the cause of our national and world problems, and who think *we* are. Distasteful? Yes. Painful? Of course. Necessary? Very ... if world peace is ever to become a reality.

Is there hope for the future of Man? Rationally, no ... but Man is not rational. There was no hope the long Cold War would end without nuclear night, but here we are ... so let us see.